Norman Craig

The Broken Plume

A platoon commander's story, 1940–45

Imperial War Museum

Published by the Imperial War Museum, Lambeth Road, London SE1 6HZ

Copyright © Norman Craig 1982
Foreword © Trustees of the Imperial War Museum 1982

Designed by Herbert & Mafalda Spencer
and printed in Great Britain by
BAS Printers Ltd, Over Wallop, Stockbridge, Hampshire

Drawings by C Dampier Freeman
Maps by John Flower

Photographs pp. 72 (top), 73 (top), 96, 97 Colonel P S Newton
Frontispiece, 99 Norman Craig
pp. 72 (bottom), 73 (bottom), 164, 173 Imperial War Museum
pp. 110, 129, 131 Major G M Jelley
p. 158 Major J S Reed

ISBN 0 901627 22 4

Frontispiece: The author in 1942

Contents

Foreword

This is the fifth volume in the Imperial War Museum's series of personal reminiscences of the two world wars and the third to be published in hardback under the Museum's own imprimatur. The series occupies a central place in the Museum's publishing programme and it is gratifying that it has been so well received, not only by professional critics but also a wider public. The titles which have appeared to date have covered the Western and Italian fronts in the First World War, the pioneering days of naval aviation and a single operation, the Battle of Arnhem in 1944. Now we have a more general account of the Second World War from the viewpoint of a junior infantry officer.

Norman Craig's elegantly written and sensitive memoir takes us from training in the United Kingdom and the Middle East to the front line in North Africa and Italy. Many of the experiences he describes will strike a chord in others who served in those theatres. At the same time *The Broken Plume* vividly evokes the special flavour of the Second World War, so different from that of the First.

The text is much enhanced by Charles Freeman's excellent contemporary drawings. Mr Freeman served with the author in Persia and Iraq, and we are grateful to him for allowing us to plunder his wartime portfolio. Thanks are also due to two other former Royal Sussex officers – Colonel P.S.Newton MBE, Secretary of the Army Museums Ogilby Trust, and Major G.M.Jelley MC – and to Major J.S.Reed of the East Surreys for permission to reproduce certain photographs from their private albums.

Noble Frankland, Director
Imperial War Museum
15 March 1982

Author's Note

This book is an account of my experiences in the army
during the Second World War. I was a conscript,
commissioned after a year in the ranks, and I served with
three infantry regiments: the Welch in the United
Kingdom; the Royal Sussex in the Western Desert, and
Iraq and Persia; and the East Surreys in Italy.

I held no staff appointments and was not concerned with
any wide issues of strategy or the planning of operations.
During the bouts of fighting in which I took part – at El
Alamein and in Northern Italy – I was totally absorbed,
like every other platoon commander, in the business in
hand and the prospects of survival for myself and my men.
For the rest of the time, as a temporary soldier with no
long-term career aspirations, I had as my main aim, when
not occupied with training or regimental chores, to derive
as much interest and amusement as possible with my
companions of the moment from our unusual
circumstances and surroundings.

The war of 1939–45, unlike that of 1914–18 in Flanders,
was one of range and movement, presenting the
participants from day to day with a kaleidoscopic variety of
fresh faces, odd locations and unfamiliar activities. I had a
full share. My experiences were not unique; they were
shared by many others who were similarly involved and
saw things from the same perspective. But such an
exceptional interlude in anyone's life deserved to be
recorded. Moreover, though all wars have much in
common, each has its own particular characteristics. I
therefore decided to recount my story, and through the
narrative to seek to convey something of the distinctive
atmosphere of those days, and of the impact of battle on the
individual soldier, which must have been essentially the
same in any war and for any generation.

I did not keep a diary, but as soon as I was invalided home in August 1945 I sketched an outline while the events and impressions were fresh in my mind; and I wrote the book during the evenings of 1946–7. The present version is substantially the same as the original, but in preparing the text for publication I have had the benefit of valuable advice and suggestions from Dr Christopher Dowling and his staff at the Museum.

Prelude

The April night was closing over the Italian countryside as the field ambulance drove slowly down the narrow road away from the front and the noise of gunfire grew fainter and fainter until it could be heard no more. There were four of us in the back: another soldier and myself lying on stretchers, a grey-haired old Italian peasant woman – cast by some accident in the path of the armies – on an upper bunk, and a third soldier, fully dressed, whom I took to be an orderly, sitting disconsolately on a stool.

Though I could not see out, it felt very safe inside. The shot of morphia in my knee had helped; but, above all, I was free from the racking tension and suspense of battle. On a small white card, pinned to the grey blanket which covered me, was an entry in a doctor's scribble, 'Gun-shot wound, right leg: compound fracture – watch circulation. Patient pale but not sweating. General condition – excellent.' The last phrase was reassuring, and I lay back to enjoy the journey.

It was pleasant enough for a time, but as the night wore on the craters and bumps in the road became more pronounced. There were inexplicable halts and starts and a lot of chattering from the driver's cab, but none of the comforting sounds outside that come from towns or villages. At one point the driver stopped, reversed the ambulance and moved off again in the opposite direction. He seemed hopelessly lost, with a fair chance of ending up behind the German lines.

We were becoming more and more restless and the atmosphere inside the ambulance was rather tense. The old lady on the top bunk began groaning and crying out intermittently in hoarse, incomprehensible Italian. Meanwhile the ambulance carried on seemingly at random along the bumpy road. I told the orderly, 'For God's sake get your driver to stop at a farmhouse and ask the way.' The soldier took no notice. Only after calling sharply to him again did I spot his heavily bandaged arm and realise that he was not an orderly at all, but another casualty. I apologised for the mistake and together we bawled advice at the top of our voices through the partition – but with no effect whatever upon the driver. All we could do was trust to providence.

At long last, after a journey of several hours, I judged from the growing noise of traffic and the hum of voices that we had reached our destination. It proved to be Argenta, the town where the battle had been fought a few days before. The ambulance halted and the stretchers were carried into some school buildings which were serving as a casualty clearing station. We were dumped on the stone floor in the entrance hall and abandoned. A cold night wind cut through the open doorway, adding to our discomfort.

A group of oafish Italian orderlies in green uniforms and feathered, Tyrolean-type hats were lounging about, bantering each other and assiduously ignoring us. After putting up with this for about twenty minutes I called out. One of them looked across and after some hesitation sauntered over. When he noticed my epaulette he gave a quick startled cry to the others, '*Ufficiale! E ufficiale questo.*' In a flash my stretcher was hoisted up and, despite my protests, swept out of the hall and propelled at a terrifying angle up a steep flight of stone stairs into a small waiting-room on the floor above.

I was moved to the next room, which was being used as an operating theatre, and propped up on a table. Several figures in white, wearing skull-caps and masks loosely tied at the mouth, converged upon me. There was a disarming geniality and heartiness in their approach. After some pleasantries a rubber band was wound around my arm and a needle with an anaesthetic injected. Someone told me to count to twenty, but by the time I reached double figures the tourniquet was released and I passed out . . .

It was daylight when I awoke to find myself lying between clean white sheets on an iron bedstead in a bare stone schoolroom. Beyond the windows was the bright blue sky, and shafts of sunlight were falling obliquely across the room. The morning was beautifully crisp and peaceful. I glanced down at my leg. To my relief it still appeared to be whole, encased in a monumental white plaster cast, which stretched from the top of the thigh to the heel, with only the tips of the toes showing.

At first I thought I was alone. Then I heard whispering and spied two young Italian girls cleaning the floor at the end of the room. As they heard me stir they turned and watched with mingled curiosity and apprehension. When I greeted them they smiled with evident relief. One of them, in pink, was uncommonly pretty, and this prompted me to wonder how badly the human frame would need to be mutilated before the imp of sex was pacified. As they resumed their work, we exchanged cordialities through the medium of my broken Italian.

A Medical Corps sergeant came in, followed by two Italian orderlies carrying a stretcher with another patient from the operating theatre. The face of the wounded man was familiar; he was an officer from the Irish Brigade who had been on a course with me at Florence a few weeks earlier. A tall, strapping young fellow, with a mop of fair wavy hair, he had been particularly dashing and devil-may-care on exercises throughout the course. Now he lay propped up on pillows, unconscious, like a white marble statue, with one shoulder bare and the other swathed in a bandage which was carried round his chest. A pad of cotton wool showing above the bandage was freshly stained with blood.

As the sergeant passed my bed on the way out he said, 'They always reckon it's nothing in the shoulder . . . but I'm not so sure. Usually much too near the heart for my liking!' He shook his head doubtfully.

In the course of the day more patients were brought into the ward. A captain, with Medical Corps insignia on his shoulder, approached the bed next to mine and to my surprise began to undress very slowly, draping his jacket over a chair. He looked at me and suddenly blurted out, 'I'm a doctor. I've been ordered to bed. They say I killed a man yesterday, but it's not true! I'm just tired, that's all.' He seemed gaunt and pathetic as he slid wearily between the blankets and buried his head beneath the sheet.

By nightfall all the beds were filled but it was almost impossible to sleep. The room was full of restless, coughing figures, each one wrapped in his own private pain and anxiety. The wounds were too fresh, the fears too recent, for there to be any comfort or cheerfulness in the place.

Next morning they prepared to move us again. This time it was a sedate and uneventful journey in the ambulance along the highway to Forli; from there we were driven out to the airfield. The stretchers were placed side by side near the runway, bathed in warm sunshine. One by one they were lifted into the waiting Dakota and hitched on to straps at the sides of the fuselage. The take-off was remarkably smooth. When we were airborne an American nursing sister in a pale blue frock came round to see us. 'Are you OK?' she asked. I watched with fascination the rhythmic movement of her jaws. 'You like some gum?' she enquired, offering me a handful of long, flat strips of spearmint. I hadn't the heart to refuse.

The aircraft winged its way across the Appenines towards Rome through the clouds and over the snow-capped mountain peaks. For me the war was over, and as I lay at peace with the soothing drone of the engines in my ears my mind went back to the beginning, five years before.

Part One: Early Days

I

I was called up in July 1940 to the newly-formed 18th Battalion, The Welch Regiment, at Monmouth. We recruits were met at the railway station and marched untidily through the streets, swinging our cardboard gas-mask containers behind us. In the dusty camp we were given three blankets apiece, a palliasse which we filled with straw from the barn, and an unwieldy bundle of khaki clothing and equipment. As night fell we trudged, heavily laden, up the hill to our billet in the old workhouse on the Hereford road.

We spent our first few days scrubbing floors and cleaning the billets for the rest of the company, who had not yet arrived. Below, in the camp at the foot of the hill, the other companies had already assembled and were living under canvas. All day long we could hear the shouts of the NCOs and the stamping and counting aloud of the men. After a few days, when the company was complete, we ourselves began training. At first it was mainly foot-drill, practised hour by hour up and down the courtyard at the end of the building, our only respite being the ritual of the 'five minutes smoke'.

Sergeant Bull was in charge of our platoon, an ex-regular from Liverpool with service in Palestine and India, now recalled for the emergency. He had a formidable appearance – lean, hard and sun-tanned – and his speech was blunt and blasphemous. He criticised our drill unmercifully and bullied us day by day with unremitting and eagle-eyed perseverance until we slowly reached a standard of precision that a chorus-girl might have envied.

Our afternoons were devoted to weapon-training, mostly on the rifle, but with occasional spells of instruction on the Bren gun. We would sit in groups in the long grass behind the workhouse, our forage caps on the back of our heads and straw in our teeth, listening to the NCOs as they explained the mysteries of the weapon. We marvelled at the vividness of their vocabulary with its inevitable sexual imagery.

After a few weeks we began route marches. In spite of the multiplicity of web equipment and the blistered feet and aching limbs, there was great satisfaction in those long marches through the glorious Wye Valley in the deepening summer. There were also occasional sunny mornings on the range when, with our stomachs pressed to the dewy turf and the acrid smell of cordite in our nostrils, we smacked bullets through the distant canvas targets. At other times we practised bayonet training with the stilted formality of the drillbook, until those few exhilarating moments at the end of each period when one by one we savaged the straw dummy with blade and butt and hobnailed boot in a burst of uninhibited ferocity.

In spite of ourselves, as the weeks passed, we began to look like soldiers. The sparkling cap badge, carefully creased trousers and shining toecaps belied the coarse khaki serge of the uniform and the clumsy ammunition boots. We were marched everywhere in neat little squads, striding through the streets to parades, inspections and other duties. Three times a day with routine punctuality we tramped to the camp cookhouse, swinging our metal plates smartly at our sides. We developed an ease of movement and a perceptible arrogance in the lift of head and shoulders. Even saluting seemed less an imposition than a welcome exercise in exhibitionism. In the evenings we would sometimes go in search of officers for practice, and when some round-shouldered specimen from the Ordnance Corps shambled by on the pavement in tactful unobtrusiveness we would stride brazenly past, feigning to ignore him until the final second when, with a sudden stiffening of the frame and a sharp 'eyes right', we would flash out a copy-book salute of quivering rectitude.

When our drill reached a sufficiently high standard we were introduced to the ceremony of 'guard'. After weeks of rehearsals and elaborate preliminary inspections of our uniforms and equipment, we assembled on the edge of the parade ground on Castle Hill and the orderly corporal gave us each a final polish with a duster. Then the adjutant and the regimental sergeant-major made their appearance and we took part for the first time in all the prancing pageantry of a battalion guard-mounting. The sergeant-major bellowed, 'Parade – as you were!' in a single breath, leaving us limp, bewildered and foolish. Next time we braced ourselves more promptly, but when the man next to me stood to attention his cap fell off. The sergeant-major stopped in front of him and bringing his face very close hissed, 'You're a nice clean soldier, sonny, but if you ever put your cap on like that again – I'll kick you in the guts!' Painfully we worked our way without further mishap through the remaining intricacies of the ceremony, in a succession of conditioned responses.

That night, after each cheerless spell of sentry duty, we rested in the cramped guardroom, a haven of camaraderie with its warm and smoky fug, profusion of blankets and everlasting aluminium dixie of lukewarm tea. At one point, as we slumbered fully dressed on the wooden boards, a German aircraft dropped a stick of bombs on the town; one exploded in the courtyard outside. The sentry, who was racing for the shelter of the guardroom, was blown with a shriek headlong through the doorway into the huddle of shapes on the floor. There was a period of some confusion until it was established that he was unhurt, and the sedate routine of the night resumed.

I had three particular companions at Monmouth: Rafferty, a college friend who had joined the battalion with me, Mendelsohn, a Jew from the Coney Island Fun Fair, and Jones 29 (identified by his last two army numbers) a soccer-playing ex-grocer from Cardiff. The four of us shared a room in the old workhouse with a handful of others. When parades were over we lounged on our beds, in collarless angola shirts and brown canvas shoes, writing letters, polishing brass buttons and endlessly boning our boots.

We argued together on every subject under the sun. The barrack room was perhaps the most complete democracy in the world. Inside ours, freedom of expression was absolute, but no extravagant or affected assertion ever passed unchallenged; there was no intellectual licence or vested privilege. Chores and other activities were arranged on a co-operative basis of scrupulous equality. We were always broke, and even the shameless importunity with which we cadged cigarettes from each other and raided one another's food parcels served to underline our essential unity and interdependence. From the common will and sympathy there

17

sprang a deep fellow feeling and a corporate identity.

Beyond, was the rest of the army. Outside the little self-protective union of friends was the jungle, the anarchy, the *sauve qui peut* of selfish individualism where the instinct for survival was epitomised in the immortal army principle, 'Fuck you, Jack. I'm all right.' With the other private soldiers in the battalion our relationship was one of wary truculence, though the bellicose profanity of our day-to-day exchanges was largely rhetorical on both sides. For despite frequent threats of violence, actual fights between soldiers were rare. We took our tone in these matters from the NCOs. Among the more primitive of the regulars it was a point of honour after any difference with a soldier to make the grand gesture, 'If any of you thinks I'm hiding behind my stripe, let him come round the back and I'll take my coat off.' The offer was rarely accepted, but it was regarded as a complete vindication of disciplinary status. Fisticuffs were the ultimate judgement, beyond which there was no appeal.

Towards authority of any kind our attitude was one of instinctive hostility, and all officers and NCOs were auto-matically suspect. Although when 'off parade' we kept out of sight as much as possible there was no escape from the tide of demands upon our time and energy, and no immunity from exploitation. Outwardly we conformed to the dictates of discipline with reasonable goodwill, but inwardly the regimentation rankled. The 'janker-wallah' became hero; each day in the dining room we gazed in awe at the group of soldiers in detention who only emerged from the guardroom under heavy escort at meal-times. These unregenerate rebels were the incarnation of our own inner revolt.

For those of us with less daring, absolution came on pay day. Pay was small – two shillings a day at first – but this was enough, with beer at sixpence a pint, to wash away in the public houses of the town the indignities and servitudes of the week. The Welch were a musically uninhibited regiment and on Friday nights the bars resounded with our tuneful rowdyism. This was the private soldier's natural element, and his triumph was complete at the end of the evening when he stood on the table-top, flushed and defiant, tunic and shirt collar open to show his independence, waving his brimming glass and singing 'Bless 'em all' in its cruder version.

After the Friday night pub crawl there was the weekly

dance. In the smoky, perfume-laden atmosphere of the Rolls Hall we competed with the rest of the battalion for local favours. Emboldened by alcohol, we even pitted ourselves against the regular NCOs and warrant officers. They were always in strength, resplendent in their 'blues' with the red stripe down the trousers, and bringing to the pursuit of their women the dedicated and ever-smiling persistence that belongs only to men who have served for long spells in isolated stations overseas. When we triumphed in these highly competitive proceedings the reward came later on the river bank. There, veiled in the privacy of the autumn mist and with an army groundsheet as a shield against the damp grass, we sought a warm oblivion. The silence of those nights was undisturbed, apart from the throbbing engines of an occasional German bomber, threading its way along the Wye towards the industrial Midlands. The bonds of our environment were completely forgotten – until a sudden recollection of the time shattered the idyll and prompted a precipitate return to camp, with a frantic sprint up the hill to reach the guardroom before midnight.

The routine of training at Monmouth was interrupted by one brief excitement, when a German invasion was reported in the early hours of a Sunday morning. We were roused from our beds and told to get dressed. The workhouse was in an uproar; footsteps pounded up and down the stone corridors; in quiet corners hoary corporals primed grenades with unconvincing nonchalance; and pale-faced recruits were sent to draw items of unfamiliar equipment from the stores.

After a good deal of confusion we were eventually marshalled outside by platoons. Major Tyler, the company commander, arrived. He was an immaculate, twenty-six-year-old regular, who dominated his company on parade and off by a masterful bearing and a boundless enthusiasm for the minutiae of soldiering. He was the best kind of regular officer, though he shared many of the conventional characteristics, such as pronouncing 'absolutely' with a minimum of consonants and 'terrific' as a monosyllable. He was in his element on this occasion as he strode up and down the ranks. When Rafferty, declining to be drawn into the general panic, asked naively, 'What exactly is going on, sir?' Tyler looked at him with incredulity before replying severely, 'We are going to fight a little war. That's all.'

Later, Sergeant Bull explained the situation in more prosaic terms. 'There's a rumour the Germans have landed in England. I don't know where and I don't know if it's true – but personally, I hope it is!' He grasped his rifle and gave a little sniff.

We marched in darkness down the Hereford road to our alarm positions and spent the rest of the night digging. At first light another man and myself were sent on a brief excursion to the range to try out the anti-tank rifle. The emergency was considered sufficiently serious to justify firing two rounds of live ammunition from the first line supply. But when we returned at midday the crisis was over, and later in the afternoon we were ordered to stand down and were marched back to our billets.

Soon afterwards a list of potential NCOs appeared on the company notice-board. It contained the names of most of the brighter individuals in the company, including Mendelsohn, but not Rafferty or myself. We held a brief indignation session. We had played our parts tolerantly and well, and it was time to put an end to this unnecessarily prolonged apprenticeship. We would see Major Tyler at once and ask for commissions. At the interview Rafferty was marched into the office first. When he came out I thought he looked a little shaken. Then it was my turn. Once inside I gave my smartest military salute and glanced down with cheerful confidence at the company commander and the array of subalterns at his back. Tyler looked up.

'You're a university man, aren't you?' he asked. 'Yes, sir.' 'An honours degree, is that right?' I nodded, and he paused for a few minutes before adding, 'Well, you know, you haven't stood out among these men as you should have done.' 'In what way?' I asked. 'Most of these men have had hardly any education at all,' he replied, 'but in an emergency – if all the officers were killed, for example – I hardly think they would turn to you for leadership.' He continued very quietly and deliberately, 'Your platoon sergeant doesn't think you are good enough for a stripe – how do you expect me to recommend you for a commission? I've spoken to your friend Rafferty and told him I can imagine him leading a very good college rag, but nothing bigger at present. Go away, both of you, and work harder. When you can convince Sergeant Bull that you are worth a stripe, I might think again.' His words would have stung less if they had been further from the mark.

That evening I was detailed as a member of an advance party for the battalion's forthcoming move to St Donat's Castle, in South Wales on the Bristol Channel coast. We left early next morning, arriving in the afternoon, and were put in tents in the woods around the castle. The rats scuttled among the fallen leaves, and not far away one could hear the sea pounding on the rocks at the foot of the cliffs. It was cold, damp and cheerless after the comparative homeliness of the workhouse at Monmouth. Three days later the remainder of the unit arrived and our platoon was moved to billets in a house in the nearby town of Llantwit Major, where we spent the winter.

Most of our days were occupied in signal training, patiently practising the alphabet with blue and white flags and lamps. As our proficiency increased we worked in pairs, sending obscene messages to each other across the countryside. In the afternoons we passed hours in the billet taking down morse from the buzzer. These activities were interrupted from time to time by unwelcome spells of fatigues in the company dining room and cookhouse at Ham House, where there were endless flights of filthy stairs to scrub and a floor black with grease to be made spotless by noon each day.

For me an unexpected reprieve came when I was chosen to attend a course for potential NCOs and, with eight other men from various platoons in the company, moved to a hut in the grounds of St Donat's Castle. There we began each day with a period of drill under the regimental sergeant-major on the concrete border of an ice-bound swimming-pool, taking it in turns to give the words of command. We were also taught the techniques of weapon training instruction and the inflexible convention whereby each lesson was prefaced with the words, 'What we're going on with now is . . .' One morning I was rash enough to introduce a variant along the lines of, 'Now, the lesson I propose to take this morning is –' I was immediately interrupted and rightly rebuked for this presumptuous originality. Thereafter I stuck to the accepted text.

By now I had grasped the key to success in the ranks – the capacity for saying, 'Yes, Corporal' and 'No, Corporal' with a humble and unvarying frequency. If this was the route to advancement, I would foot it with a will. When I rejoined the platoon after the course, it was occupying another billet: a dilapidated house with dismal black-out screens, frozen pipes and blocked lavatories. I was appointed 'private soldier in charge of the room', which meant assigning barrack room tasks to the others. It was clear that my military future would hang on the results. By good fortune, the group was a naturally cooperative one and with a certain amount of persuasive encouragement from me the room and its occupants soon established a high reputation for smartness. Before a battalion quarter-guard we often spent as much as thirty-six hours cleaning up, and for the kit inspections, which were normally held on Saturday mornings, we went to even greater lengths. The cleaning was done on a communal basis: one man scrubbed the floor, another boned the boots and a third cleaned the overcoat buttons and polished the plates and mess tins with Silvo, which completely ruined the next day's meals. Sometimes we laid out our kits on the bed overnight, and on one occasion I even induced the others to join me in sleeping on the floor to avoid disturbing the display. I was quite desperate by this time.

In early spring there were rumours of another move, and one day we were ordered to prepare for a journey to Spalding in Lincolnshire. We travelled overnight by train and in the early morning marched through the town to our billets – wooden huts in a field belonging to the local high school.

At last I was rewarded with a stripe and made section commander in the long hut where ten of us lived. The weather was still confoundedly cold, with frost and some snow. We had a coke stove which we always stoked up until it was red-hot at night, so that those whose beds were near it had to move over to the centre of the room to avoid being roasted alive. Every crack and hole in the windows and door was carefully sealed to work up a tolerable fug, but by morning we were always frozen. It was purgatory to wash and shave at the exposed ablution benches, which stood in the middle of an open field. Very often the fire bucket was put to communal use instead, but the room was always spick and span for inspection in the morning, and the standard of turn-out flawless.

At Spalding several battalion church parades were held. We were always rigorously inspected beforehand by the company commander. On one occasion he suddenly gave a cry from the centre of the ranks: 'Put this man under open arrest, sergeant-major – he hasn't shaved.' There was no mistaking the horror in his voice. We shared it.

The atmosphere inside the church was tranquil and soothing. As we sat in the quiet pews we became quite oblivious of the army; even the sermon seemed an intellectual feast after the plainness of our daily conversational fare. One morning at the conclusion of the service the organist, seeking an escape from the solemnities of the Anglican ritual, burst rebelliously into the Prelude to Act 3 of *Lohengrin*. Entranced, we walked slowly down the aisle and through the arched doorway into the churchyard beyond.

We lined up under a clear spring sky ready to move off. A gentle breeze whispered among the beech trees and sunlight danced on the leaves. Suddenly the voice of Sergeant Bull rang out in all its fury. 'Stand STILL! I'll bloody shake you up, lad!' His blasphemies resounded among the speckled gravestones, circled around the dreaming spire and re-echoed in the startled ears of the departing congregation. Instantly we were recalled from the world of spiritual enchantment to hard physical reality. It was a complete reassertion of the secular authority over the ecclesiastical.

A number of impressive ceremonial drill parades also took place at this time. The elaborate cleaning up beforehand was tedious, but when the process was completed and our toe-caps were shining like glass, our equipment spotless and our rifles proof against even the most meticulous examination, we faced the inspecting officer with arrogant assurance. After the preliminary inspection we were marched to the football field where compact detachments of men from other companies were converging from all directions, their rifles glinting in the sun and the rough brown of their khaki uniforms contrasting with the deep green of the web equipment. The road echoed with the rhythmic tramp of hobnailed boots and the gruff, cryptic injunctions of the platoon sergeants. For ten minutes pandemonium reigned on the field. The NCOs, jockeying their platoons into position, seemed to be seeking to deafen each other with their discordant cries. Then the hubbub gradually subsided into complete silence. The cautionary command was given and the ranks stiffened. The battalion was called to attention, and in a brief formality the colonel took command of the parade. Then came the absolute submission to a single will, the complete obedience to the word of command. In that mass subservience there was an element of ecstasy, a strangely joyous satisfaction. There was something of the Nazi in all of us.

As spring advanced and the weather improved we began to practise manoeuvres as a battalion in the neighbourhood of the town. The surrounding countryside by then was ablaze with multi-coloured blooms. Dazzling arrays of daffodils, tulips and hyacinths stretched towards the horizon in seemingly endless rows. In the morning whenever we halted and lay down to rest on the banks of a dyke we could hear skylarks singing and see them soaring upwards through the haze towards the open blue sky; in the late afternoon when we turned back to camp the whole landscape would be framed in the crowning magnificence of an East Anglian sunset.

But the terrain was quite unsuitable for training. It was impossible to advance across the fields because of the bulbs and flowers, and we were not allowed to use the dykes because they were full of water and our turn-out would have been ruined. So we were reduced to trundling unrealistically down the middle of the road. In these artificial conditions we had to have almost as many umpires taking part as troops. To make matters worse the roads in Lincolnshire were heart-breaking. We would turn a corner on the march and there, stretching implacably before us as far as the eye could see, would be the dead-straight, monotonous ribbon of the road. Sometimes, peeping above the horizon and looking like a matchstick, a solitary church spire would be dimly visible, indicating our distant destination.

At Spalding I was given an interview for a commission. I was expecting a gruelling inquisition, but the board consisted of two people only, the major, second-in-command of the battalion, and the regimental sergeant-major. The former was quite affable. 'What do you do with your spare time?' he asked. 'Sometimes I go to the pictures, sir, sometimes I read.' 'Oh you read, do you? What sort of books do you read?' I pondered for a moment and then replied, 'Poetry, chiefly.' 'Poetry!' he grunted, 'that's pretty dry stuff, isn't it?' The sergeant-major regarded me meanwhile with a look of undisguised contempt and asked, 'Do you play any games?' 'I've played rugger for the battalion,' I hastened to mention, and that raised my stock a little. 'Has your father got any money?' the major asked. 'A bit,' I said guardedly. 'What I mean,' he added 'is that if you got into a scrape, would he help you out with a fiver?' Though the question seemed to betray a certain lack of confidence in my reliability as an officer – if I ever became one – I mustered a plausible enough reassurance on the point and was spared any further interrogation. The major closed the interview by saying that I would be told the result in a week or two.

The following weekend we had orders for another move to an aerodrome at West Raynham in Norfolk. There we lived in overcrowded bell tents. It was a triumph of ingenuity to fit ten men with their kits into each tent. The drunks were a trouble late at night, but we managed. The RAF food and amenities were admirable and the days passed pleasantly enough, despite depressing newspaper headlines about the fall of Crete.

Soon afterwards we moved to a second aerodrome, at Coltishall. This was a fighter station, with Hurricanes leaving day and night on operations. Now and then we wandered round the hangars, vaguely hoping to meet a few pilots and to talk to them in philosophical terms about the problems of life and death, with which we rather naively imagined they must be preoccupied at this time. We never succeeded. Meanwhile the only opportunity for distinction which came our way was some elaborate ceremonial drill on the handsome RAF parade ground. Apart from that, we were kept busy with routine guards at various points on the perimeter of the airfield. The worst of these was the Main Gate Guard, which involved wearing full equipment for twenty-four hours, even indoors. Between spells of sentry duty we solaced ourselves with continuous pontoon, which we kept going on a shift system.

One Sunday morning we lay in our barrack rooms as reveille sounded, relishing the luxury of an extra half-hour in bed. Tousled heads appeared above the blankets, and matches were scratched as cigarettes were lit. The room was stuffy and stank of beer. Someone opened a window. The fresh June air streamed in, carrying the sounds of a wireless from next door. We were listening with one ear when the seven o'clock news came on. The announcer began, 'This morning units of the German army crossed the Russian border . . .' Russia was now in the war, on our side. A great cheer rang through the building.

When we were not on guard there were very few duties. On sunny mornings during physical training periods we used to run down the lane for a couple of miles to the river for an unofficial plunge. In the evenings there was a collection of inviting country pubs to visit, an occasional dance, or walks in the woods with the WAAFs. War could not have been further from our thoughts, though there was always the drone of the returning fighters and the sight of their silhouettes against the sunset to remind us of the unrelenting struggle that was raging elsewhere.

Eventually, in July, the news I was waiting for arrived. I was to report to company headquarters in a nearby village and be ready to leave in a few days for an officer cadet training unit. On my last evening I went back to the aerodrome to say goodbye to the others. They were on guard duty. There is a bluff sensitivity about farewells between soldiers, for there are no loyalties stronger than those between close friends in the ranks of the army. When I left that night I felt the separation keenly, even though a commission had been my constant aim from the very first day.

2

The OCTU was in a requisitioned holiday camp at Heysham Towers near Morecambe. There were about a hundred of us on the course. Soon after our arrival the chief instructor addressed us, pointing out that our projected elevation to the rank of officer, assuming we passed the course, would be of a temporary nature only. Disarmingly, he urged us to avoid, during that brief period, doing anything likely to damage the reputation of those whose association with the army would be more lasting. His conclusion, however, was not discouraging. 'No one,' he said, 'is thrown out of here except for misbehaviour, or complete idleness,' – which did offer the possibility of just scraping through.

The cadets came from a wide variety of regiments and were readily distinguishable by their headgear. The Guards contingent, consisting of a few foot-stamping sergeants and one erstwhile warrant officer of frightening dignity and military omniscience, wore smart round caps with the peaks almost touching their noses. A group of former tank men with dour faces and unsteady legs, had black berets pulled well over the right ear. A handful of pale-faced and long-haired intellectuals from rifle regiments, still dazed from their rejection by a motorised infantry OCTU, wore green side-caps perched very straight on their heads. The ebullient Scots as usual sported their motley range of bonnets and tartan glengarries in any way they chose. The remaining cadets from the miscellaneous county regiments made do with standard forage caps, balanced at varying angles and each with a distinctive badge. Only the shining white capband was worn by everyone, to denote our new-found status and common objective.

Training was mainly by day, but partly by night. We were usually transported in fifteen-hundredweight trucks, huddled in the back with rifles on our knees, along a wind-swept road to the wooded hills around Carnforth, north of Lancaster. Here we practised the gamut of infantry manoeuvres prescribed in the tactical manuals, by platoons and by companies, with each cadet taking it in turns to command. After each day's exercises there was a post mortem on individual performances in the lecture hall. To sit waiting for such personal criticism, always delivered in agonising detail, was an excruciating experience.

Our free evenings were spent poring over training pamphlets on rickety bunks in the chalets, or gossiping in deep leather armchairs in the lounge to the strains of *Finlandia* and *The Waltz of the Flowers*, which alternated relentlessly on a deafening radiogram.

The course lasted four months. It was an invigorating and instructive period, though the enjoyment was tempered by the ever-present fear of being thrown out. Occasionally the axe would fall and three or four men of the company would be returned to their units. In most cases they were obvious failures, but occasionally a surprise victim was included and then everyone was in a flutter. However, the period of suspense slowly drew to a close, and discreet visits were made to Austin Reed's in the town for our service dress fittings. Sam Browne belts also appeared furtively in a few chalets and the more confident cadets began polishing them in anticipation.

When the final day of the course arrived early in October 1941 we crowded into taxis for the station, wearing our immaculate new uniforms complete with leather gloves and carrying the small swagger stick, which was the hall-mark of the newly-created subaltern. I had been posted to the 2/5th Welch Regiment, at Brighton. I wrote to tell them the time of my train. At the station a polite driver was waiting for me. 'The truck is outside, sir. May I carry your bag?' he enquired.

At company headquarters, which was in a requisitioned house, I met the officer whose platoon I was to take over. He was just leaving with the weekly pay for the men and invited me to join him. The platoon was billeted in an old school building at Patcham, on the outskirts of the town. It was growing dark when we arrived. A trestle table with a couple of hurricane lamps had been set up in the entrance hall and we pulled up a chair alongside the colour-sergeant, who was seated behind a bundle of acquittance rolls. The men, who were already lining up in the background, had come straight from work and were still in muddy denims. At first sight I found them a bit disappointing, and it was hard to believe that they would turn out to be personalities as lively as Mendelsohn and Rafferty in the old platoon. They were cheerful enough, though, as soldiers always were on a pay parade, stepping forward briskly to get their money, and saluting twice – before and after – in the drill I knew by heart. As I studied them in the lamplight I began to take to them more and more, and looked forward keenly to getting to know them all in the weeks to come. Yet it did not need the expression of polite circumspection on their faces, as they eyed me sitting there with my elegant greatcoat unbuttoned and service dress hat thrown casually on top of the colour-sergeant's papers, to tell me that from now on I was well and truly on the other side of the table.

I had dinner that night with the company commander and the rest of the officers of 'C' Company. Everyone was particularly kind and friendly. The beer was good and there was an enormous fire. I learned that the role of the battalion was coastal defence and that our own company was in reserve. In the morning I would be taken to the rolling downs behind the town to inspect the alarm positions, a set of trenches cut deep in the chalk and buttressed with fascines. I did not spend long at Brighton with the battalion, however. There were just a few days' training with the platoon, an officers' cocktail party and a game of rugby against the Navy – a week in all – and then, as was often the lot of the newest arrival at a unit, I was chosen for something which nobody else wanted, in this case an advanced infantry assault course at Lochailort in the Western Highlands of Scotland.

I travelled throughout the day to Glasgow and from there, with several other officers similarly bound, caught the train for the West Coast at five in the morning. When it grew light we found ourselves passing through remote and desolate mountain country with the wind whistling around the carriage windows. At Fort William we changed to a smaller two-coach train, which ran westwards as far as Mallaig, alongside the 'Road to the Isles'. Lochailort was about thirty miles along the line, on the edge of a loch surrounded by sombre, craggy mountains. We marched from the station to the camp, a group of Nissen huts in the grounds of Inverailort Castle. Our beds were in the huts but the mess was in the castle itself.

Soon after our arrival we were paraded by a tiny Scots officer, who doubled us to the quartermaster's stores where we were each issued with a couple of canvas fatigue suits. In a breezy voice he announced, 'You can get out of your pretty clothes, gentlemen, we're going to start moving.' That afternoon we went for our first mountain climb. Though it was not a long one, it was sufficient to lay several officers low.

Western Scotland has the heaviest rainfall in the British Isles, and it rained almost continuously throughout the course. Every day we returned from training soaked to the skin. Of our two fatigue suits, one was always in the drying room.

Lochailort was the prototype of the battle schools, which later had such a vogue in England. The pride of the place was its obstacle courses. Considerable ingenuity had gone into the construction of these obstacles and every conceivable device, natural and artificial, was included. Over these you had to double with full equipment and a rifle. The courses were constantly waterlogged so that, having successfully neg-otiated one fiendish obstacle, you arrived exhausted on the ground, only to sink up to your knees in a bog on the way to the next. At the end of one of the courses was a cliff-face which had to be climbed by rope. The rope was always shiny from the boots of those who had gone before, your own clothing saturated and your hands slippery. One day we were floundering exhausted at the foot of the cliff, attempting to gain a hand-hold. The commanding officer was standing at the top, attired in glittering service dress. 'You've got no guts, you clap-stricken buffoons,' he shouted. Someone looked up and swore back at him with equal coarseness. 'Well done that officer,' responded the colonel, 'that shows spirit!'

The instructors were competent if rather theatrical. One little man always slept in a bivouac on a lawn in front of the mess, although it was December. Most of the others had their own diligently cultivated idiosyncrasies, which were calculated to impress the students. They imagined they were the last word in swashbuckling virility. Our valuation of them was a good deal less flattering.

The programme was full, varied and exacting. We did practical map-reading in the hills, although there were few convenient landmarks to help us. We carried out opposed landings from the loch and were sniped at with live ammunition. We practised street fighting, mess-tin cooking and unarmed combat. Those who were not completely exhausted by the day's work spent their leisure hours doing yet more mountain climbing or shooting deer.

The course concluded with a three-day exercise based on the famous march by Montrose from Kilcumen to Inverlochy. We were driven by night to Fort Augustus. Laden with full equipment, weapons, ammunition and food for the journey, we began at first light the slow climb along the Tarff valley, through a forest and across the snow-covered mountain range, in mingled spells of hail, snow and sunshine. Descending in the afternoon, we followed the path through Glen Roy and made for Roy Bridge in a long trek lasting until after nightfall. There, in a wooden hall, we cooked our oatmeal and pemmican, a form of concentrated beef extract, changed our soaking socks and slept for a while in our gas capes on the floor. We were roused in the early hours for a night march across the moor towards Fort William, and a dawn attack on the ruins of Inverlochy Castle. Then we headed back for Lochailort. After a painful and monotonous tramp along the shores of Loch Eil, and a night in groundsheet bivouacs beside the burn at Glenfinnan, we reached camp at noon the following day. In all we had covered seventy miles in two and a half days; not in itself an epic journey, but something of an endurance test all the same. It was too much for some of the students, who fell by the wayside to be picked up later by transport.

The physical side of the course was admirable and most of the instruction was sound. Lochailort was mercifully free of the morbid crudities which obsessed some of the divisional battle schools that were modelled on it. At one school I heard about later, loudspeakers blared out hate slogans, such as 'Remember Hong Kong' and 'Remember Singapore', and the commandant took the students to a slaughter-house and threw sheep's offal over them to familiarise them with the sight and stench of blood. This artificial attempt to inculcate a fighting spirit, to imbue the soldier with an eagerness to get at the enemy and tear him to pieces, was a nonsense. A pugnacious disposition, natural or cultivated, was very little help in action, as anyone who came within a mile of an angry German or Japanese soon discovered. For the spirit of human aggression has a magical tendency to evaporate as soon as the shooting starts, and a man then responds to two influences only – the external discipline that binds him and the self-respect within him that drives him on.

When the course finished a few days before Christmas I travelled by train to rejoin the battalion at Weymouth, where they had moved in the intervening weeks. To my delight, in the New Year the CO asked me to organise a hardening course modelled on Lochailort. With a group of selected NCOs I was to take each company through for a week in turn. This kept me busy during the day; and at night there were routine patrols in the frosty moonlight along the meandering cliff-top paths between Weymouth and Osmington Mills.

In February we moved to Poole, where the company was lodged in some scattered requisitioned houses and the officers in a block of flats called the White Lodge. Here a normal pattern of daily training and mess life was resumed, though this was interrupted from time to time by several large-scale exercises. These were carried out on a divisional or corps basis to enable us to practise our counter-invasion role, and lasted three or four days at a time. They normally took the form of a long initial move by road, followed by a sequence of infantry manoeuvres by day and night on the ground. In the course of this activity the battalion covered the whole of Dorset and part of Hampshire including the New Forest, and Wiltshire as far north as Marlborough. In the process we gained within a couple of months a more detailed topographical knowledge of the area, and closer intimacy with the countryside, than many of the locals probably acquired in a lifetime.

A few days after each exercise it was customary for a conference to be held in some local cinema. The divisional or corps commander presided and it was always quite a social event. Here the hierarchy of the division assembled with all the pomp and ceremony it could muster. The cinema was always carefully laid out, with detailed notices telling everyone exactly where to sit. Sergeants sat on one side of the aisle and junior officers on the other, the front rows being reserved for senior officers. Well to the fore were the commanding officers, and in front of them the brigadiers and generals, whose bald heads did not seem half so impressive as their glorious crimson hats.

The conference always began with an account of the exercise, given by the Brigadier General Staff from Corps, an immaculate officer in a gleaming Sam Browne belt. He narrated in dramatic detail the incidents of the exercise, reading from a stack of typewritten notes resting on an illuminated lectern. Beautiful diagrams were flashed periodically upon the screen and a bored-looking major with an enormous pointer listlessly indicated the place names as they were mentioned. By the time the brigadier had finished, most of the sergeants and a good many of the junior officers had nodded off. Then the corps or divisional commander came forward on the stage to review the exercise. The commanding officers remained awake and politely attentive; they had more to answer for. The conferences served their purpose in providing some measure of coherence to the exercises as a whole. One gained such a fragmented impression while taking part.

In April I was sent on another course for junior leaders, at Bournemouth in the Sandbanks Hotel. This was much closer to the normal tradition of officers' courses than the one in Scotland had been, and was more gentlemanly and academic. There was, it is true, an assault course, which the staff had been trained to refer to in tones of suppressed horror; but it was a trivial affair really. We were only required to go over it once every four days and, after Lochailort, could have done it blindfold. In the afternoons there were lectures. We were given a printed précis of each lecture to spare us the tedium of taking notes, or even of staying awake. Several people fell asleep during the afternoon lectures, an easy thing to do on a sunny day after an active morning in the open and an ample lunch.

Outdoor demonstrations were more popular, for the fresh air kept us alert. Sporting shooting sticks, field glasses and map cases, we strolled about with the air of potential military geniuses. There were numbers of TEWTs (tactical exercises without troops) during which we were presented with problems requiring a theoretical solution. Since there were no actual troops and – more important still – no live enemy, one always chose a dynamic solution to show the required spirit of well-bred aggressiveness. The secret was to make one's answer bristle with a fair sprinkling of popular military clichés, such as 'having a look see', 'pooping orf' and 'sorting out the Hun'.

There were a number of outside speakers. On one occasion Brigadier Templer lectured to us. His talk was called 'The Junior Leader in Battle', or some such title. He began by saying, 'There is an old tradition that there should be no shop talked in the mess. I never want to hear you talk anything but shop, at any time. We have all got so much to learn, gentlemen, and there is so little time.' Some students thought this rather spurious, but I did not see it that way. The brigadier was quite serious. In the eyes of this unswerving regular, the sacrifice of so powerful and sanctified a professional convention was an act of considerable symbolic importance: total war with a vengeance.

He went on to describe a subaltern's first experience of battle. 'You are advancing peacefully with your platoon along a quiet lane. Suddenly all hell is let loose. You look up, and your platoon sergeant's guts are hanging on a tree beside you. The platoon is turning to run – it is then, gentlemen, that you must *grip* those men.' He paused in absolute silence and, holding out his arm, tightened his fist slowly to give graphic illustration to his words. It was superb theatre and we sat enthralled.

When I returned to the unit a brother officer, Bill Beecher, and myself were ordered by the CO to take the recruit company, who had just finished their initial training, on a week of battle-drill at Studland Bay. This was sheer enjoyment, for recruits were always keen and free from the usual contempt for training which one found among soldiers of some two or three years' service. We bought walking sticks, grew moustaches and made a point of getting unnecessarily muddy and wet to impress the recruits. We were, in fact, aping the battle school instructors, and probably looked just as ridiculous.

When the day's work was over we were still bursting with energy. We wandered among the sand dunes, throwing bakelite grenades into derelict beach huts, firing rifles and revolvers unreasonably close to each other and playing with every explosive we could lay our hands on. It was all very childish but nevertheless a natural part of one's development as an officer. In the evenings we used to paddle an assault boat across the bay to a tiny cove and, after tying up and climbing the cliff path, make for the Bankes Arms. We would return with dusk falling across the bay.

When the recruits had gone our own company moved to Studland Bay, a delightful area where we spent a perfect month in Knoll House, a requisitioned luxury hotel close to the sea. The duties were light. At dawn we would begin with a patrol on foot along the deserted beach to comb the sandy foreshore, sunlit and freshly-washed, for any tell-tale débris of German reconnaissance raids. Apart from this and an occasional company or battalion exercise, there was only a little light training and preparation for guards. The June weather was especially indulgent and the company spent most of their time swimming and sunbathing. We had the place to ourselves. The coast at Studland, because of its vulnerability to enemy landings, was a 'protected' area and the beach was out of bounds to civilians. The minefields on the dunes and the scaffolding at the low-tide mark along the shelving shore were no deterrent to the men, and the free run of such a superb expanse of sand was a rare privilege. We made the most of it and soon became as brown as berries. Studland had a further big advantage in its remoteness from the rest of the unit. Battalion headquarters communicated with us by ferry, which did not run after six o'clock at night; this kept us safe from interference. The village was like an island – a company commander's dream posting.

Yet there was an air of unreality about our lives at this time. The training exercises were vigorous enough, but all-too-obviously simulated. The TEWTs we took part in around Swanage, where the main body of the battalion was stationed, were highly artificial notwithstanding their ingenuity. We talked battle-drill by the hour in bloodthirsty terms, but that was about all. The comfort and security of our billets were always awaiting us at the end of the day. Quite a few of the married officers had their wives staying with them in hotels in the neighbourhood, and every evening the bars were crowded with customers in bright dresses and well-cut uniforms. In sharp contrast, the morning newspapers were full of the ding-dong battles in Libya, and this made military life in England seem more and more of a sham. I told the adjutant one morning that I would not mind a posting overseas. The opportunity occurred within a week.

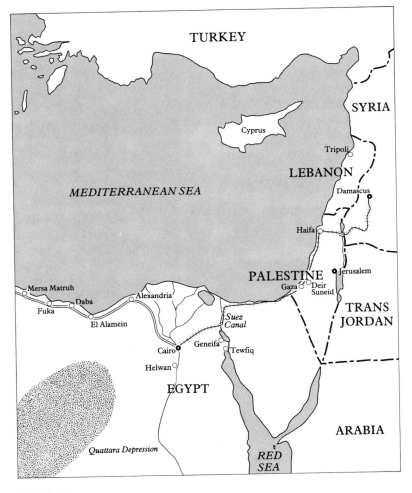

Middle East, 1942
Scale one inch = 150 miles

Part Two: The Western Desert

3

My two weeks' embarkation leave passed all too quickly. At its close I duly reported to Gravesend to pick up a draft of soldiers from the Durham Light Infantry who were to travel with me. In Shorne Camp there was little to do for the next few days except fuss over our newly acquired tropical kit and brood. In the evenings each glass of beer had an added relish and one's appreciation of every feature of the countryside was quickened. This was Dickens country – the Thames marshes in front, and behind them the rolling Kentish landscape. It seemed particularly beautiful in July 1942 but invested with a veil of melancholy.

After a week of waiting, orders to move arrived. We were bundled into three-ton trucks, which rattled off to the railway station as the cool summer evening closed around Gravesend. We slept through the night in our special train, reaching Liverpool by morning. At the dock we caught our first glimpse of the SS *Samaria*. Long columns of troops with their topees and kit bags beside them were waiting alongside. Any wistful regrets I might have had about leaving England were rapidly dispelled in the general turmoil on the quay. There, a troublesome soldier under sentence, who had been belatedly attached to our draft, began to show a marked disinclination to complete the journey. He had to be handcuffed to two other soldiers as a precaution. What with watching him, keeping the draft together in the milling crowd, and looking after my mountain of personal baggage, I had more than enough to think about. Consequently, when at length the word came to embark and I had finally succeeded in shepherding the last of the men up the gangway, the poignancy of my own parting steps on native soil was quite lost in relief at getting safely on board.

I took the men down to their mess deck and then hunted for my own quarters. They were a converted ship's cabin with

37

bunks for six officers and I quickly made myself at home. The evening meal in the officers' dining room was superlative, and the wine and cigars plentiful and cheap. The auguries for the voyage were good. The *Samaria* sailed in the middle of the night.

Next morning and on succeeding days there was a 'boat stations' parade in life-belts, but no other duties for officers. We passed much of the time reading in our cabins, while the decks outside resounded with the stamping feet of the men's physical training class and the interminable echo of housey-housey. Evenings were usually spent in the smoky lounge, where little cliques congregated: the cavalry officers in their long stylish jackets, the astonishingly youthful subalterns from the rifle regiments and the would-be-intellectual doctors. Perspiring waiters passed to and fro with drinks between the crowded tables. In the background a piano was sporadically thumped by a few amateurs. The range of music was limited but these plaintive repetitions had a certain haunting nostalgia. The room rang with the noise of laughter and the clink of glasses; while down below, the engines with their ceaseless pounding hurried us inexorably on.

As we approached the tropics the heat in the cabins became intolerable; the humidity was such that our khaki-drill shirts and shorts were always wringing wet by the afternoon. We changed into clean slacks and tunics in the evening, but the dining room was stifling and as soon as dinner was over we would escape to the open boat deck. There, beneath a firmament of unfamiliar stars, we found a cool relief in the night air, lulled by the gentle pitch of the prow as it surged through the glinting phosphorescent waters. The lower deck was usually crowded with troops, sitting in the dark and singing quietly and rather sadly to the accompaniment of a guitar and an accordion.

The threat from U-boats was always present and we travelled in a convoy of about a dozen ships, escorted by a light cruiser and two destroyers. We had made a wide detour around the north of Ireland into the mid-Atlantic and continued on a zigzag course through the tropics. As it happened, there was not a single scare throughout the voyage; which was just as well, for I could not bear to think what would have happened if we had been torpedoed, such was the overcrowding on board. The men's quarters were densely packed. The only furniture in the gloomy messdecks was the long benches and rows of plain wooden tables, where food from the galley was dished out. At night hammocks were strung up side by side from hooks fixed to the low ceiling. They covered every spare inch of space, even the area over the mess tables. The congestion was bad enough in itself but in the tropics the sweltering heat and suffocating atmosphere turned the place into an inferno. Apart from occasional spells on the cramped troop deck above, the men were confined below, playing cards, reading or scribbling letters – clad only in shorts and canvas shoes, with perspiration streaming off their bodies. They had precious little sleep at night in these conditions, which were aggravated by the noise and heat from the engine room immediately beneath them. It was a horrible journey for them.

A fortnight's sailing brought us within sight of Freetown. There was great excitement as we approached land, but the *Samaria* anchored in the bay and we had no chance to go ashore. Soon the convoy struck south again. Off the Cape of Good Hope we encountered the highest seas of the voyage and in the rough, cold weather were glad to change back into battledress. Once round the Cape, things improved and the seas abated. On reaching Durban we were delighted to be told to disembark. We were moved by train to a large transit camp outside the town and for three days savoured the celebrated South African hospitality in civilised comfort before returning on board. On the morning before we sailed a hospital ship on its way back to England moored alongside us. The troops gathered along the deck rail and gazed down at the cargo of cripples and invalids. This unexpected encounter had almost the shock of physical impact.

The journey up the coast was more rapid. The danger of submarines had lessened and the ship no longer zigzagged. We anchored off Aden for a night, before passing into the Red Sea. It was hotter than ever, and impossible to sleep in the airless cabins, so we took to sleeping outside. This meant an early reveille, for a surly seaman, with bare feet and turned-up trousers, watered the decks with a hose at first light – and he was no respecter of rank or persons.

Though we had assumed as much from the start of the voyage, it was not until this late stage that we were told our destination was Egypt, where the Eighth Army, after the disastrous reverses of the early summer, had taken a stand at El Alamein, some sixty miles west of Alexandria. No wireless broadcasts had been allowed on board ship for fear of submarines, but once a day a summary of the BBC news was pinned to the wall of the lounge. From these bulletins we had followed with some concern the course of the renewed German assault in the desert at the end of August. But the attack had been repulsed. The Nile Delta was safe, at least for the time being, and conditions appeared fairly normal when we finally anchored at Port Tewfiq.

Orders were given for the disembarkation. The lighters – dirty, rusty, ramshackle barges – drew alongside. Kits were thrown in and we scrambled aboard. At the quayside a train was waiting. The carriages were a discoloured white, with shutters instead of windows, bare wooden seats and a faded map of the Delta for the allurement of the tourist. As the engine drew out, we had our first sight of Egypt – the back streets of Suez. Trains, by their very nature, seem to seek out the most squalid slums in any city. Suez was no exception, but the usual filth and stench were magnified a hundredfold. Whenever the train creaked to a standstill, the corridors came alive with hordes of dusty, tattered children, garrulous hawkers and plaintive beggars. At length we passed into flat open desert.

We were bound for the Middle East Infantry Base Depot at Geneifa on the Suez Canal, half-way between Suez and Port Said. It was a large camp in a sandy plain and consisted of four or five square miles of solidly packed tents, neatly spaced in rows. Here and there stood sprawling tin erections – cookhouses, messes, cinemas and shelters for the fat, pampered contractors, who sat in monopolistic comfort behind their stalls. The ground was sand, which had been flattened down and hardened in the roadways by the constant passage of vehicles. In front ran the Suez Canal, a dismal expanse of dirty water fringed with a few date palms and shrubs; behind, relieving the monotony of the plain, rose two sandy hills called the 'Great Flea' and the 'Little Flea'. The sky was cloudless and blue. Day followed day of bright, hot, inescapable sunshine.

From the train we were driven in lorries through the camp to the officers' mess for a meal. The building was a big, corrugated-iron structure swarming with officers from every infantry regiment in the army. The atmosphere was distinctly robust and it was every man for himself in the jostling mass at the dinner table. Depots had a way of bringing out the worst in officers: the courtesies and inhibitions of regimental life seemed to vanish. Geneifa was no exception and was clearly not a place to leave a wallet lying around. But, above all, the camp brought home to one a sense of insignificance and expendability. One was nothing more than a cypher, a routine replacement for someone at that very moment being killed or wounded at the front.

There were all sorts in the mess, ranging from wounded officers – limping, bemedalled and patronising – impatiently waiting to get back to their regiments even at the risk of their lives, to the other extreme, the hangers-on and scroungers who seemed to have been at the base ever since it was established, always managing to avoid a posting. The older inhabitants wore tailored bush shirts, well-laundered slacks and desert boots of bright brown suede with rubber soles. They carried fly-whisks and had leather covers over their wrist watches to keep the sand out. They conversed in the conventional idiom, with frequent references to 'sprogging up' and 'up in the blue', invariably hailed each other with the Arabic greeting '*Sayida*', and asked eternally, 'What's the griff?' Yet, strangely enough, when we joined an infantry battalion in the line later, we found the officers wearing standard khaki drill uniforms with army boots and conversing in normal English, blissfully untutored in the prevailing fashions.

Among our new companions in the depot the talk was all about the 'big push', which was likely to start any day now. I had half expected to find a spirit of defeatism in Egypt after the reverses earlier in the year, but there was no trace of it here. Regularly each day a typewritten list of names would appear on the notice-board; there would be an uproarious burst of singing at the bar later in the evening; then, in the early morning, when the valises had been rolled outside the tents, another small band of officers – almost unnoticed – would disappear 'up in the blue'.

For the rest of us there was very little work to do. We did some token physical training daily and occasionally we put on our equipment and went with the men for a scramble-cum-walk across the hills at the back. This was called a hardening course, intended to accustom us to the climate, but it was a sensible, casual business. Not that it mattered, for the worst of the summer was over and we became acclimatised without difficulty. Sometimes we undertook a formal route march, which was a little harder for it took us out into the noonday sun.

In the afternoon the officers' lido bus would call. This plied between the mess and the officers' club, a square flat-roofed building of white stone on the shores of the Suez Canal. There was bathing in the canal, and coffee and afternoon tea in the lounge. Each day one saw the same faces here, the same bronzed Apollos and their few, languid girl friends, having a glorious war. One night there was a dance. We arrived suitably inebriated after consuming a fair number of cans of iced American beer. But with a couple of hundred other tipsy males milling around it was impossible to get near the dozen or so nursing sisters. After several unsuccessful attempts we trekked back to camp along the sandy path which ran between the irrigation channels, ostensibly disappointed but chuckling to ourselves as we practised direction-finding by the stars.

There were also the camp cinemas, the property of a notorious contractor. These were large bare tin shacks with rows of wooden benches and a few collapsible chairs at the back for capitalists with fifteen piastres to spare. The projector was worked by Egyptian operators. The film usually began upside down and when this was righted the reels were often shown in the wrong order. The dialogue was American and the film was overprinted in French at the bottom, in Greek down one side, and in Arabic down the other, the picture itself being barely visible beneath the maze of intriguing characters. There were frequent breakdowns and each time the audience cheered wildly, except when the last prolonged and irremediable stoppage occured; then they would rise as one man, smash the seats and depart in the best of humours. The contractor always accepted this development with the bland, fatalistic indifference of the Orient. 'Maleesh,' he would no doubt say to himself. 'What are a few dozen wooden benches anyway? I make a fortune, so why worry?'

One night, amazingly, there were no breakdowns. It was an American film of the mid-thirties about a group of intrepid pilots in a South American airline. The hazard of occasional crashes in the course of their employment gave them the pretext for a lot of blasé behaviour and their beautiful girl friends the excuse for some highly neurotic outbursts. The hero of the film made a fetish of always scrounging matches, on the grounds that it would be wasteful to buy a box in case he was killed before they were all used. I was struck by the irony of it all. Here were a couple of hundred real soldiers, being primed daily for a holocaust in which many of them would be killed or mutilated. Yet they sat there totally absorbed in this utterly bogus film.

Late one evening, eight of us were unexpectedly given notice to move into the desert early the following morning, to act as umpires in an Eighth Army exercise. The prospect of a pleasurable preview of the fighting without much risk was most attractive as we were already heartily sick of the base depot. At first light we put our tin boxes in the store, packed a small bed-roll and suitcase apiece and after breakfast clambered into the back of an open fifteen hundredweight. As the truck scorched along the Cairo road across the flat wind-swept desert, we sat clutching our hats with a welcome breeze playing in our open shirt fronts and in the legs of our shorts.

By midday we reached Cairo. We were impressed by its size and vigorous activity, and surprised by the modern appearance of the city centre and the large, splendid shops. We had only an hour to spare and made for the Gezira Sporting Club for lunch. There we sipped iced beer on a shaded verandah, served by obsequious, coal-black waiters with red tarboosh hats and flowing white gowns. Around the swimming pool lay several girls in bright bathing costumes, while a powerful sun-tanned hero dived spectacularly into the sparkling, green waters. To us this was the last bastion of comfortable elegance before the unimaginable rigours of the desert. I could not help feeling a bit out of place but consoled myself with the thought that Lawrence of Arabia would have felt equally uncomfortable in such surroundings.

After lunch we took the road northwards along the Delta from Cairo to Alexandria. This busy road was the vertebrae of the Eighth Army. It was one continuous flood of forward traffic: impetuous staff cars, half-assembled aeroplanes, tanks on transporters and stolid, unhurried convoys of ration and ammunition lorries – a heterogeneous, ill-assorted mass with a single destination. Our rendezvous was point 156 – a numbered milestone, just past the 'Half-way House', a well-known landmark. We arrived late in the afternoon and pulled off the road to wait for our guide. It was growing dark when he appeared. Over the horizon, emerging from the sandy waste, a tiny jeep became visible. We watched it draw closer, zig-zagging to avoid the bad patches of soft sand. Our guide jumped out to meet us. He was a happy-go-lucky captain, wearing a black beret, scruffy, sand-covered suede desert boots, corduroy trousers and a dirty crumpled shirt. With his puckish, casual manner, unhurried polished drawl and wide, innocent blue eyes, he displayed that tinge of affected insouciance which was the characteristic of the desert type.

I said I was sorry if we had arrived late. 'Don't worry about that, old boy,' he replied. 'You kip down here for the night. I'll go back to Div HQ and pick you up here first thing in the morning. No use your coming tonight. You'd get stuck.' He climbed into his jeep, which was loaded with petrol tins, water cans and brewing-up kit, and buzzed away across the desert like a large, skittish bumble-bee. We watched him disappear on the western horizon, a pin-point against the crimson setting sun. We drove the truck a little further off the road and rigged up a shelter. The sun sank swiftly and in a few moments it was quite dark, with all the arbitrary suddenness of a desert nightfall. Then we made our first desert brew: a cut-away tin full of petrol-soaked sand was lit and the overflowing brew-can pushed into the flames. By the time we had finished the night sky was alive with stars. We lay down to sleep in our valises on the sand as a cold, rising wind whipped across the flat desert.

Our guide arrived at first light. He pulled up alongside, hailing us cheerfully. His batman, with brusque, professional competence, set about lighting a fire for breakfast, while the captain capered around the jeep with a razor and toothbrush, performing his ablutions precariously on the bonnet. I was pathetically unorganised, with no mirror or basin, and I threw myself on his charity. 'Help yourself, old boy,' he said as he thrust into my hands his battered bowl, a twisted, splintered driving mirror and a thin slab of soap in a tobacco tin. 'You clean your teeth in the water first and shave in it afterwards,' he explained.

When breakfast was over we drove off at right angles to the

road straight into the desert. At this time the line at El Alamein was static and held principally by the infantry. A fair portion of the army, including most of the armour, was in reserve midway between the front and the Alexandria-Cairo road. Although on the map it looked as though the troops were compressed into a small corner of Egypt, that was not how it appeared on the ground; for once off the main road one was in the open desert. Even a whole army could occupy only a fragment of this vast expanse.

As we drove westwards our truck frequently stuck in soft patches of sand. We had to jump out and push until it was clear, while our good-natured guide circled around in his more manoeuvrable jeep. The going gradually improved and soon we came upon hard, recognisable vehicle tracks in the sand. As the sun rose higher the heat increased and a haze appeared across the desert, crystallising here and there into the occasional, shimmering mirage. After a few hours we reached a large cluster of evenly dispersed vehicles. This was the headquarters of the 10th Armoured Division. We drove into the centre of the group and parked beside an armoured command vehicle, where the guide dismounted. We waited.

Ten yards away a colonel sat on a 'thunder-box'. This was a simple wooden soap box, with a gap cut in the top and a movable lid. You dug a shallow hole in the open sand, planted the box over the top – and there was your latrine. When you moved away you threw the box on the truck and filled in the hole. Nothing could be simpler. Here in the open, under a relentless sun, sat the colonel, placidly attending to the demands of nature and casually flicking away the flies with a whisk. He was lost in thought and quite oblivious of our presence. The thunder-box was the symbol of the informality of desert life.

A staff captain told us we were to be split up and attached to separate brigades in the division. We would be called together again shortly for the forthcoming exercise, but in the meantime were to gain desert experience with individual units. Another officer, Lieutenant Howe, and myself were dispatched to the 133rd Lorried Infantry Brigade, which we found by following a compass bearing for several miles across the sand. Brigade headquarters was in the centre of the area, with the vehicles methodically spaced around the armoured command vehicle, which was distinguished by its red pennant. We joined the brigade just as it was finishing an exercise. Normally this would have been a bad moment to arrive but in the desert it made no difference; one time was as good as any other. We were greeted cordially and invited to join the other officers for a meal. The brigadier lined up in the queue for supper with the rest of us.

In the morning the brigade moved back to its normal location. The move was carried out in desert formation, the drivers signalling to each other with their mirrors and maintaining set positions; the troops in the back of the lorries were fully dressed and armed, ready to spring into action at a moment's notice. By midday we reached our destination, a spot where the ground was a little more worn and where a few piles of stones and a flimsy hut gave evidence of previous occupation. At a distance of about a mile in each direction from brigade headquarters lay the three Royal Sussex battalions, the 2nd, 4th and 5th. After reporting to the 2nd Battalion Howe and I were sent to separate companies.

4

I spotted company headquarters – two stationary vehicles and a few buff-coloured bivouacs detached from the rest – and drove across in the truck. The only figure I could see was a man standing naked in an improvised bath of petrol tins. He was soaping himself and singing cheerfully. It was the company commander, whose name was Campbell.

'Hello,' he called out, 'Come and sit down. You must excuse me – this is a dreadful extravagance. We're down to two water bottles a day, but the "Q" has scrounged a bit extra.' He fired the usual string of questions put to a new arrival, about England, the trip out, the base depot and Cairo. His batman handed him some clean slacks and a bush shirt. He dressed carefully. We sat down on a couple of upturned crates and the batman walked over to the cookhouse to fetch our meal. It was an enormous steak, beautifully cooked, with tinned potatoes and peas, and followed by tinned peaches and canned milk, with a large mug of hot, sweet, desert tea.

The sun dropped and by now the evening was refreshingly

cool. We sat and gossiped. The company was waiting for the three-ton truck to return from Alexandria with NAAFI supplies. It came bouncing into the company area just before dark. We feverishly off-loaded the crates of beer, tore them open and scattered the straw and shavings in the sand; then we piled up the bottles, tins of fruit, cigarettes, soap and razor blades into convenient stacks. The men of the company came up and drew their rations by torchlight; each man paid for his little bundle in tattered Egyptian notes or metal piastres and rushed away to his bivouac. This was a night of merriment.

The company commander's utility truck had been converted into a mobile headquarters. The flaps at the back were pulled down to preserve the black-out and an inspection lamp was fitted up to provide lighting. We crowded onto the wooden seats inside and indulged in a private orgy. We had canned beer, bunches of bananas and a pile of racy, colourful magazines from Alexandria, as well as one or two of those ill-printed, illiterate, pornographic masterpieces in which the Levantine cities excelled and which had their own unconscious humour. With all the smoking and drinking in this cramped, stuffy space we soon became quite light-headed.

When we tumbled out into the fresh air, the company commander seized a rifle and fired five joy rounds into the sky. The others kneeled down and wriggled snake-like into their bivouacs. I had no bivouac. My valise was rolled out at random in the sand, open to the night and the sky; and with the breeze brushing my face I fell asleep.

Next morning there was a battalion training exercise to rehearse a rapid assault against lightly organised resistance. The objective was the White Hills, two dreary hummocks breaking the flat monotony of the desert south-west of the battalion position. I travelled in the company commander's utility truck and we motored up to the start while the mortars pumped smoke onto the objective. The company leapt out of their lorries and attacked through the smoke, firing live ammunition. On the way back after the exercise the troop-carriers became stuck in the sand, and everyone inside had to get out and heave and shove until they were clear. This was a common sight in Egypt – a stubborn, overloaded truck, flanked by a scrum of grunting, sweating soldiers. The sand was a great leveller, striking at the vehicles of the mighty and the humble alike.

That afternoon there was no work to do. I sat against my bed-roll and read, in the persistent company of the eternal flies. In the evening there was a discussion on the exercise. The NCOs squatted round the company commander in the sand and a thousand and one detailed problems were discussed. The young corporals, fresh and eager-faced, had a fine challenging spirit. In that company there was no friction at all between ranks.

The next week passed in much the same way. By day there was training, and afterwards in the quiet of the reddish-gold sunset an hour of smoking, gossip and reflection. There was a rare freedom in this life, to which the openness of the desert, the mobility of the unit and its isolation all contributed. The battalion, though operating from a fixed location, had a nomadic capability which enabled it to move, fully equipped, at a moment's notice. Petrol seemed to be plentiful, with none of the 'petrol-less' days and restrictive work-tickets that had made things so irksome back in England; and the training exercises ranged over a very wide area. At the same time the outside world had for practical purposes ceased to exist, and there was never a stranger to be seen. The only contact was the mail, which arrived when it chose to, and the one airmail letter card, which was all each soldier was permitted to send home weekly. Units were dependent upon their own resources. The men had to find their own amusements, which they did without difficulty, clearly revelling in this environment, in which they were spared most of the petty controls and minor harassments of more conventional military surroundings. Everything that had to be done was directed towards eating, sleeping and preparing to fight.

Health appeared to be good and the daily sick parade was sparsely attended. There were no mosquitoes and no fevers or colds; only Gippy-tummy, the violent and racking diarrhoea which struck at everyone in turn for a few days. This was an embarrassment rather than a danger. There was one unfortunate incident in a neighbouring battalion where the adjutant, an extremely regimental officer, was obliged in an emergency to drop his trousers in the middle of his own improvised parade ground in broad daylight.

The main drawback in the desert was shortage of water. The daily ration of two pints per man was beggarly in the intense heat. There were occasional 'rackets', one of which was to send back an organised party on a clandestine trip to Prince Omar Tussin's well, which was in an old monastery near the Cairo road and offered unlimited supplies. When the trucks returned later, piled high with overflowing jerricans, the whole company had a ceremonial bath. Normally, personal water bottles, which held a pint, were filled first thing in the morning and this allowance had to last all day; most of it went for drinking and any that could be spared was used for shaving or washing clothes. The second pint of each day's ration was kept by the cooks for making tea.

Tea was, in fact, the great blessing of desert life and brewing up something of a ritual. The most impressive brew of the day was the early morning one. There was a rule that no fires could be lit before sunrise, but well before then most people were stirring around their vehicles. Tins full of sand were soaked in petrol and the brew-cans placed on top. Impatient soldiers stood by, matches in hand, waiting for the go-ahead. More often than not, before the signal could be given, someone succumbing to temptation would toss a lighted match into the petrol, to be followed immediately by all the others so that the desert was instantly aflame, while admonitory figures in staff cars tore helplessly around.

One morning Howe and I, along with the other officers from the base depot, were called to divisional headquarters, where our next task was explained to us. We were not to be umpires after all, but traffic control officers in an exercise to practise moving the division through a minefield. We were likely to be called on to perform a similar role later on, when the actual offensive took place. The divisional exercise began the same day when, after a cursory briefing, we were driven out at dusk and dropped off at control points on the lanes, which had been specially marked in the sand. We each had a telephone and a signal orderly. That night it was pitch-black and columns of tanks and tightly packed troop carriers came thundering past. They took most of the telephone wires and a few of the phones with them. It seemed a disorderly shambles; yet, at first light, by some indefinable magic, all the vehicles contrived to be where they were supposed to be – on the other side of the minefield – and each man was in his proper place.

After a couple of days back with the unit we were summoned to Brigade, given a pile of maps and a truck by the brigade-major and sent off to corps headquarters, which was at Berg Al Arab near the main coast road. Here we were to see a rehearsal of the traffic control arrangements for the forthcoming offensive. We drove eastwards as far as the Cairo-Alexandria road and then turned north. At Amariya we forked westwards, halting at the junction with the coast road to brew up under a clump of date palms. In the afternoon we continued westwards. The sand on each side of the road was almost pure white, stretching into the distance in rolling, finely rounded dunes. Away to the north lay the blue expanse of the Mediterranean.

Berg Al Arab was recognisable by its squat, 'Beau-Geste' fort. We turned down a rough track, seeking our objective in the maze of dispersed and camouflaged vehicles. As we moved from one to the other making our enquiries, a rising wind began to tease the loose sand. In no time a veritable sand-storm arose, sweeping all before it and darkening the sky. We drove on slowly and painfully, the flying particles biting into our faces as we huddled on our valises in the back of the open truck. Another officer, who was in the cab with the driver, fared no better, since windscreens were not fitted in the desert for fear that they would glint in the sunlight. Soon we were all smothered in sand, and could only see a few yards ahead. However, we reached the command vehicle at last and installed ourselves nearby.

We improvised a shelter with a vehicle tarpaulin, but the sand seeped in everywhere, filling our hair, eyes and mouth. When at length the wind abated we prepared a meal: bully beef stew, tinned fruit and oatmeal biscuits plastered with tinned butter and marmalade. Everything was covered with a layer of gritty sand but we found it palatable enough. Suddenly rain began to fall in large deliberate drops, the first I had seen in the desert. We stood about in it gleefully as it soaked our shirts and covered our bare knees with trickles of sandy mud.

By morning the sun was shining again and after breakfast we joined the rest of the officers at the appointed rendezvous. In the plan for the battle it was the intention – in the interests of surprise – that the armour should stay well back in an assembly area some ten miles or more behind the front until the night of the attack, when it would move forward under cover of darkness along six parallel tracks. In the rehearsal these tracks were simulated by lengths of coloured scrim laid across the sand. At a given signal a number of soldiers, each carrying an empty petrol can to represent a unit of transport, were to walk slowly along the tapes, while the traffic control officers at designated posts en route reported progress by field telephone to a token divisional headquarters. It was an ingenious model for its purpose, but before a start could be made with the exercise a message came that it was cancelled, with no explanation given.

For a time we stood around chatting and swopping anecdotes with a batch of officers from 1st Armoured Division engaged on similar duties. We had prised out of the staff at Corps an unofficial hint that the battle was to begin within a week and we speculated light-heartedly on our likely part in it. Having talked long enough to ensure that it was too late to get back to our units in a single day, several of us took it upon ourselves to break the journey with an overnight stop in Alexandria.

It was an exhilarating excursion. On the outskirts of Alexandria we passed the reeking *abattoir public*, teeming with the Egyptian poor – gaudily dressed men and drab, black-veiled women. Squat, wooden carts loaded with stone slabs, rumbled like tumbrils on their solid wheels. The pavements were packed with noisy, scrambling natives. Nearer the city centre our truck was caught up in a stream of milling traffic: overflowing trams with their trumpet-blowing conductors, speedy taxis with frenetic drivers and a mass of miscellaneous military lorries. After parking the truck, we wandered through the streets, admiring the women in their bright cotton frocks and the large European shops. We bought soap, toothpaste, toilet bags, torches and all the other things that our brief foretaste of the desert had taught us to be so necessary. On the strength of a fortnight's apprenticeship we masqueraded as real desert types, with our crumpled shirts and caps bleached with a deposit of fine white sand. Later in the Cecil Hotel we sipped long, iced John Collinses as we listened to the drunken braying of a major from the 51st Highland Division, and marvelled at the skill of the gilly-gilly man, the dexterous Arab conjurer performing at the bar.

Early next morning we took to the road and after a while headed once again across the open desert to rejoin the division. Landmarks were few and far between, and the confusing tracks could only be identified by occasional black tar-barrels, painted with white alphabetical symbols. We followed our track to the divisional area, but when we arrived it was empty; in the several square miles, hitherto crammed with vehicles, there was nothing but bald, bare desert. The evidence of recent occupation – the charred, discarded bully beef cans, the worn track ruts – seemed merely to emphasise the desolation of the place. Yesterday there had been an army here; today there was nothing. We felt the sudden sense of impotence and panic which one experienced when lost in the desert, and drove vainly around looking for a clue.

At last we spotted a single, isolated truck. The divisional signals officer was reeling in cable. He explained that the division had moved the previous night to a forward assembly area. He gave us a map reference and a compass bearing – meagre comfort to such novices as ourselves. Suddenly he had a brainwave. He believed 133 Brigade had left a rear party at their former location. Sure enough, we found a dozen scattered vehicles. It was late afternoon when we reported to the transport officer in charge of the rear party. He told us that the division had moved straight across the desert to a forward concentration area, avoiding the more usual line of approach along the coast road. He suggested we stayed with him overnight and rejoined the battalion together next day.

In the morning we drove north-west across the desert, the leading vehicle navigating by sun compass. As we moved deeper into the interior the sand became harder and the formation of the ground changed. It became much darker, in places quite black, and was broken up by patches of craggy rocks. In the middle of one of these we came upon the battalion, leaguered in the usual way, though the bivouacs had vanished and blankets were spread loose in the sand, ready for a quick get-away. Howe and I found a niche at battalion headquarters near the intelligence truck.

That evening the CO, Colonel Hooper, and the intelligence officer came back from the army commander's conference at Cairo. Rumours were quick to circulate: the offensive was due to start in three days' time and the orders would be given out next day. In the morning the battalion was drawn up in a hollow square. A large-scale chart of the battle area was set up in the centre. We were called to attention and stood motionless in the desert sun in the clear early morning air, rows of men in clean khaki drill with polished boots and shining cap badges. The formal ranks looked totally impersonal, responding with disciplined correctness to the commands. But each man was anxious and attentive.

The colonel stepped forward, young, lithe and athletic. He spoke in a friendly, confident manner, beginning with the words the army commander had used the day before: 'The battle now about to begin will be one of the decisive battles of history. It will be the turning point of the war . . .' He explained that it would be a 'dog-fight' for ten days and then a 'bus ride to Tripoli'. He unfolded the general plan for the initial phase of the battle, which was to be an assault by four infantry and two armoured divisions, of which 10th Armoured was to be one. The exact role of the battalion was not yet known, but it would be committed on the second or third day.

Here was a group of men, of friends, untouched as yet by the plague of war, about to be thrust into the carnage. The battalion was quite ready for battle, and in a corporate sense eager to be blooded and to put into practice against the enemy the lessons so patiently rehearsed in the past months. It was as though the guns and rifles, begging to be turned towards a human target, had slowly gained mastery over their owners and were driving them on in spite of themselves. Yet I could sense the quiet, suffering reluctance of the individual soldier. I would not be with the men in the battle and as a mere spectator felt like a trespasser, intruding into the privacy of their thoughts at a moment when they were incapable of artifice.

When the parade was dismissed I was conscious of a sense of anti-climax. Somehow, the grandeur of the occasion had been missed. Perhaps a fiery harangue in the manner of Shakespeare's Henry V had been called for. Then I realised that behind the prosaic simplicity of the colonel's presentation there lay a wealth of cool and courageous resolution. At a time like this the fighting man respected only lucidity and directness in speech. Any display of wordy and artificial rhetoric would have been as much out of place here as it would have been at the real battle of Agincourt.

In the afternoon Howe and I were sent to the forward assembly area; the rest of the battalion was to follow under cover of darkness. The route, we were told, would be marked with petrol tins spaced at intervals across the sand. But when we drove out of the battalion leaguer we encountered a sea of empty petrol tins and abandoned brew cans. The early vehicles had contrived to flatten most of the really necessary ones, so that it was quite impossible to discern the way. However, we carried on as far as the main divisional axis, where the route was marked with little red 'foxhead' signs – the symbol of the division – and we followed these.

We slept near brigade headquarters and in the morning surveyed the scene. The whole division had arrived during the night. The desert was a mass of vehicles, tanks and guns. Weeks before, large numbers of canvas covers, simulating tanks, had been erected in concentrations throughout the area. The divisional armour was now parked under these covers so that the latest forward movement would not attract the attention of enemy reconnaissance aircraft.

A truck arrived to take the traffic control officers to their allotted posts. The six approach lanes, which were some three hundred yards apart and ran from the assembly area to the front line, were clearly defined. The sand had been hardened by the passage of vehicles. Hurricane lamps in cutaway petrol tins were mounted at intervals on cairns of stone. When the initial attack was launched the lanes were to be extended through the British and German minefields as soon as sappers – following hard behind the assaulting infantry – could clear the necessary gaps. The tanks would then pass through and deploy over the open ground behind the forward troops.

10th Armoured Division was allocated three lanes and we were dropped off at key points along them. My post was near the start of a lane called 'Boat Track', close to an intersection with a lateral track known as 'Charing Cross Road'.

My signaller, Private Climpson, and I were planted in the middle of nowhere, with a telephone, blankets, a brew can and a sandbag full of rations. We began to dig our slit trench beside the telephone. Away to the south on an adjacent track I could make out another of our little detachments fixing a makeshift shelter over their trench. To the north nothing was visible, for some rising ground cut off from view all activity between there and the coast, which was about two miles away. Boat Track was dead. Hardly a vehicle passed. We lay in the sand all day. In the afternoon a staff officer arrived in a jeep and gave us our instructions. The battle was to start next evening at twenty minutes to ten; we were free until then.

As the sun rose on the morning of 23 October we fried our tinned bacon and beans on the petrol-tin fire, rounding off the meal with hard biscuits and jam. Stocks were low, however, and I decided to make a foraging expedition. There was another even stronger temptation. Never had we been so near the sea. It was an opportunity that could not be allowed to pass. After the dry, hot, blinding sand, the ration of two tepid water bottles a day, and the dusty grittiness of clothes, blankets, food and belongings – after all that – the Mediterranean was like a fantastic dream. I arranged by telephone to meet one of the other officers at Charing Cross Road and together we hitch-hiked to the coast.

We jumped off at the main metalled road and hurried across the soft, white sand dunes. Over a low ridge we sighted the Mediterranean. We threw our clothes down on the sandy shore and ran into the fresh inviting waves. The calmness from a distance was an illusion, for here the sea was high with swift, foamy breakers that struck against one's middle. It was an exquisite, shocking coldness. Afterwards we lay refreshed upon the beach and dried ourselves in the burning sun. We were quite alone on that solitary stretch of shore, which was soundless except for the rhythmic beating of the breakers. Reluctantly we turned our backs upon this paradise and plodded over the dunes to the busy high road, with its unrelenting flow of traffic, its brisk, officious, red-capped policemen and its battered signpost that read 'To El Alamein Station'.

On the way back I called at corps headquarters. Approaching the cooks' wagon – a large camouflaged caravan – I spoke to a cook-sergeant who was standing on the steps. He was an enormous man, naked to the waist, with brawny, tattooed arms. I explained my predicament. We were in an isolated traffic control post with short rations and were unlikely to get any more during the battle. Perhaps he could spare something for my signaller and myself? The request was completely unofficial. The sergeant said nothing, but quietly filled a sandbag from his store of tinned food, even including a loaf of fresh bread. He handed me the sack without a word. It was an act of pure Christian charity. I was very touched and ran back to the control post in triumph.

It was the evening of the battle, and as we cooked our meal in the fading light there was not even a muffled crump from the front. Soon we began to hear the distant, whining rumble of approaching tanks, as column after column slowly eased its way out of the assembly area. The heads of the columns halted at Charing Cross Road, which was the starting point for the forward movement to the line. A jeep cruised up out of the darkness through the deep ruts, casting a shower of fine, powdery dust behind its back wheels. I could faintly make out a tense figure at the wheel. He leaned forward and in crisp, quiet tones said, 'The brigade is lined up at the start point. We shall cross at 2142 hours. It that quite clear? – 2142.' I thanked him and asked, 'Who are you – a liaison officer?' 'No! The commander,' he snapped. Then he threw the jeep into reverse, turned round abruptly and sped back to his column.

The time was half past nine. The tanks behind had come to a standstill and it was quiet everywhere. There was a full moon, but a few fleecy clouds covered it momentarily and dimmed for a while the clarity of the night. The minute of the opening barrage approached. Suddenly, a second before time, a single battery of guns fired a salvo. It was like a racehorse which, unable to endure the suspense a moment longer, had leapt forward a fraction before the remainder of the field. The noise of this premature salvo had scarcely sounded when there was a low, flickering rumble across the desert and the sky was lit with flash after flash, like sheet lightning, illuminating the sand with a ghostly yellow incandescence; the desert rocked and roared from end to end as the western horizon became suffused with the brick-red glow of exploding shells. From out to sea there were flashes from naval vessels as they pounded the shore and bombers droned overhead towards more distant targets. In the German lines a succession of Very lights soared into the sky, painting plaintive distress signals on the impassive night. The battle of El Alamein was on.

For the first time I was watching an army's artillery blast its way into a live target. I could visualise the panic in the enemy's slit trenches, the ringing telephones and frantic cries for help, the chaos and the mutilation. There was a majestic fury in the barrage and a pitiless violence in the guns. Such spectacular and deliberate savagery left me breathless. This then was war. It was a thrilling and disturbing moment.

5

There was little time to ruminate for the first vehicles were already bearing down on the control post. My main task was to identify each unit as it passed, which usually involved yelling at the leading driver. Only trucks were allowed to use the middle of the prepared lane; tanks were expected to follow a parallel path some twenty yards to the side to avoid tearing up the roadway with their tracks. The plan was to stagger blocks of transport and maintain regular spacing between individual vehicles. But in the dust and darkness, and with the inevitable hold-ups along the line, everything rapidly became bunched together. Quite often I found myself trapped between two continuous columns – thundering tanks on one side, and troop carriers and mixed transport on the other. I did my best, through Climpson and his telephone, to keep Division informed of progress by the columns.

The flood of traffic continued unabated all night long and at daybreak we were still busy at our post. The advance had played havoc with the road, which was cut in deep uneven furrows. Teams of negroes from the Pioneer Corps were rushed around in lorries and rendered yeoman service, filling in the ruts with stones and levelling the surface. Our artillery maintained its bombardment throughout the morning, though it was now really a series of separate shoots against individual targets. Overhead RAF bombers roared by at regular intervals, giving a heartening impression of power. The news from the front was that the infantry battle was going well. By midday the movement of transport at our control post had slackened, and by late afternoon was no more than a trickle. That night we were able to get some sleep – with one interruption. An isolated enemy aircraft, the first I had encountered since landing in Egypt, dropped a stick of high explosive bombs nearby, which shook the desert and woke us up but did not seem to have hurt anyone. Next morning the track was clear and the place was a backwater once more.

Lieutenant Lacey arrived from his control post, which was over the ridge to the north. He was a tall, angular character who had been a battle school instructor in England. He seemed keen to take part in this offensive; it was an important battle which ought not to be missed. He suggested we should jump on a passing carrier on its way to the front, find a congenial infantry unit and try to persuade the CO to make use of us unofficially. It was a giddy, quixotic proposal, but I admired him greatly for making it. We were giving it serious thought when news arrived that we were all to be collected in a truck, taken to divisional headquarters, which was now established well forward near the original front line, and issued with fresh instructions. Lacey returned to his post.

We followed the bumpy track towards the front, picking up other traffic control officers en route. This took until nightfall. It was a slow painful ride to divisional headquarters with sudden, exasperating jolts that shot us cursing into the air. We had to pass through the gun-line – the heavy and medium artillery which was drawn up behind the headquarters. Few things could be more unpleasant than such a journey in the back of a three-tonner along an unfamiliar route at night. From every side came violent and bewildering explosions, which sent the truck shuddering across the track. Brilliant flashes momentarily lit up the road, revealing here and there the stark outline of an angry 'medium' with its bustling gun-team, before we were plunged once again into total darkness. At last we came upon a ring of vehicles by the roadside. The tiny, red lamp of the command vehicle shone from the centre of the group. We reported to a staff captain and were told to make ourselves comfortable for the night.

In the morning I was dispatched in a truck to find Howe, the last of our party, who was still at his post further forward on the edge of the minefield. As we passed Hammam station a formation of Stukas swooped down. The RAF had gained dominance over the battlefield by this time and Stukas held less terror now for the troops. Within seconds the whole desert was ablaze with retaliatory fire. Every weapon in the Eighth Army seemed to be directed towards the enemy, firing wildly and inaccurately into the sky. The anti-aircraft guns pumped away, ringing the target with clusters of exploding shells; streams of tracers from the Brens shot upwards; each individual, however inadequate his weapon, seemed to have dropped what he was doing and to be shooting away with rifle and revolver. The practical effect might have been negligible but the moral effect was tremendous. Suddenly someone by whimsical good fortune rather than design scored a hit and a

Stuka burst into flames. Fascinated, we watched as it sank gracefully to the ground, belching clouds of black smoke. We were so absorbed that we failed to notice four other Stukas which were bombing the road behind us. I could see figures on each side of the track ducking for shelter and heard warning shouts from the back of the truck. But we drove on with the perverse and dogged fatalism that sometimes overtakes one. The raiders passed and we were unharmed.

Howe and his signaller were waiting at the opening to the minefield gap. It was now a quiet locality; yet two nights earlier he had slept there, just before the battle started, in a position closer to the enemy than any other man in the army. He told us of the confusion and panic on the night of the attack. The advancing vehicles came to frequent halts; frenzied staff officers roared up and insisted upon overtaking; column commanders demanded priority and ignored instructions to wait. Soon there were two or three separate columns driving side by side through the narrow gap and by morning there was a solid traffic jam. It presented such a perfect target for shelling and bombing that some impatient drivers were tempted to back and pull off into the open desert. They managed to cover a few yards, but then with a sickening roar the sand lifted from beneath them and the vehicles were stranded high and dry.

On the return journey we passed the first batch of prisoners. A shabby, timid band in their white peaked caps and grubby drill tunics, they looked very different from the newspaper photographs of the victorious German army in France. We stared at them with curiosity as they shuffled by. The soldier is by nature of his calling a proud figure made for parades and colourful display. He is ill-fitted to the lowly condition of defeat. There was something embarrassing and unnatural about these broken, silent men.

Back at the armoured command vehicle the staff captain appeared preoccupied. A tank battle was in progress and he was busy intercepting messages on his set. As each bit of information came through he marked it up meticulously on the map. For him it was detached and entertaining business. We could follow the proceedings on his noisy earphones. Two casual voices were in conversation: 'Hello Baron . . . hello Baron . . . A couple of Mark IIIs have just come over to 867292 (or some such reference) . . . Breeze over and see them off, old boy . . . Johnnie to Baron . . . over.' 'Hello Johnnie . . . hello Johnnie . . . I'm all tangled up in wire at the moment . . . How about you going over to deal with them? . . . Baron to Johnnie, over.' And so it went on. It is the monstrous paradox of modern war that the most violent exchanges often take place to the accompaniment of this conversational jargon.

When the wireless traffic subsided the staff captain removed his earphones and descended from the vehicle. He was plump and debonair and spoke in a thin, foppish voice. He explained that our job as traffic control officers was now over but he realised that we were 'just dying to get into the big party'. We would be attached as liaison officers to the various brigades, where we could see the battle at first hand. The alternative, though he as good as dismissed the idea, was to go back to the base depot. It was a cheerful offer, and a comfortable enough prospect for him, I thought, as I watched his batman carefully lay out the sheets on his safari bed and prepare to cook a large plate of meat and vegetable stew.

Two of our party, nonetheless, elected to go back to the base. The rest of us were distributed fairly summarily among various units in the division, including a gunner regiment. Howe and I were sent back to 133 Brigade.

Howe was from a machine gun regiment. He would have been quite justified in returning to the depot to await a posting to a specialised unit, but so far as I could tell the thought never entered his head. He was not remaining out of bravado but because he would have been quite ashamed to turn back at this stage. He was a quiet, diffident fellow, gentle in manner and refined in speech, with none of the pushy ebullience of the typical infantry subaltern. He had, in fact, been an art student in Chelsea and could have been totally out of place in this environment. Oddly enough, as was often the way with his type, he had adapted himself admirably to the conditions of desert life, enduring its trials and discomforts with amused tolerance.

Rear brigade headquarters proved to be quite close and there we hunted out a staff captain who undertook to run us to advanced headquarters next morning. We found a deep, safe-looking pit with room for both our beds and made ourselves comfortable, talking until well into the night on every conceivable subject except the war.

In the morning we climbed into the back of the staff captain's truck and were driven through the minefields – and for miles and miles beyond it seemed. We were surprised by the extent of the advance. We passed regiments of field gunners, stacking their shells and digging emplacements, their bare bodies and steel helmets gleaming in the sun. Squadrons of tanks were deployed beside the track ready to be called forward. Here and there was a captured enemy post, with an occasional stiff, grey corpse draped over the sandbags, and a pile of bedraggled looted kit – gas masks, weapons, clothes and magazines – scattered around. From time to time we passed the scorched hulk of a tank or the derelict chassis of some burnt-out truck. There were even a few aircraft, the splintered bodies of crashed Messerschmitts, each with the intriguing black cross on the side.

Further forward the vehicles became thinner on the ground. As we drove slowly to the top of a slope we came upon brigade headquarters, the familiar circle of trucks with a command vehicle in the middle. From here one could survey the whole battlefield in a vast sandy valley beyond. On a ridge opposite two tanks were blazing bright and red on the horizon. Just as we arrived a liaison officer drew up in a jeep and called out to the brigadier: 'There's still no sign of the Fourth, sir.' The brigade had made an attack the previous night: one battalion had overshot its objective and vanished. It was extraordinary that it could disappear in this wide exposed plain, where one would have thought it impossible to hide a single man. But the whole battalion had swept off through the darkness and had not been seen since. The brigadier shrugged his shoulders.

Howe and I were directed to an empty slit trench and told to wait there for instructions. At one stage we passed some time browsing through a bundle of captured documents with the brigade intelligence officer. But for the most part we felt neglected and unwanted. Periodically a few isolated shells came whining overhead and burst well to the rear. Sometimes one would drop short, with a screeching whistle and a flash, and we would bury ourselves in the sand.

At length the brigade-major emerged from his command vehicle. He seemed tired and overworked, with that look of strain that men have in battle, living as they do on their reserves of nervous energy. He seemed delighted to see us.

'Very glad to have you. The CO *will* be pleased!' he said, quickly dashing any wild hopes we might have harboured of a privileged existence at Brigade as liaison officers. 'But we can't send you both back to the 2nd Battalion. Howe, you can go back to the 2nd – and you,' he turned to me, 'can join the 5th.'

An officer from the 5th Royal Sussex, Captain Lee, had just arrived at brigade headquarters. He was not returning immediately but said there was a sergeant waiting in a truck nearby who would drop me off at the unit. I bade a hasty cheerio to Howe, who was sitting on the edge of a slit trench. Then I boarded the truck. The sergeant moved over and began to start up. Suddenly there was a violent explosion as a shell burst in the middle of the track in front of the vehicle. The blast shook the cab and smothered it in a shower of blinding sand. We both scrambled hastily out. We were unscathed and to our surprise the truck was undamaged. But as the sand cleared I heard a frightened, ghastly whimpering from beside the command vehicle. It was Howe. He was half kneeling, half hanging out of the trench, clutching his stomach. A sharp red stain had appeared on his shirt front. He was bending forward, writhing in agony, and his eyes were wild with pain and terror. 'It's my guts . . . Oh my guts!' It was a startled, hopeless cry, like an animal's; there was something deep and incommunicable about the extremity of his suffering. A shell splinter had caught him in the chest as he knelt over the edge of the trench and torn its way into his abdomen. He was sobbing deliriously.

The staff captain spoke to me. 'It's your friend,' he said. 'He's been hit!' 'Has he?' I answered in a tone of detached brutality. Every ounce of sympathy seemed to have dried up within me. I could not face this spectacle. All the anxiety and dread of the past weeks came welling up within me. I felt tense and taut. I knew I could control myself but only by a slender thread. I turned away. All my life I shall be ashamed of that moment of bleak indifference to a man's suffering. The staff captain, although he was outwardly far more shaken than I was, tried to persuade Howe to lie still and began placing field dressings on his stomach.

I went to fetch help. I raced two hundred yards along the track to a first aid post belonging to the Highland Division. A doctor was standing outside. 'A friend of mine has been hit,' I

explained. 'Could you possibly come and have a look at him?'
'I can't leave my post,' he answered. 'There's a battle raging
out there.' He had a coarse voice with a pronounced Scottish
accent and made a showy gesture with his arm towards the
front, where a single flicker of red tracer was pencilled across
the growing darkness of the night. The pettiness of his
attitude infuriated me. 'But you can have a stretcher party
and carry him over here,' he added as an afterthought. I
seized on this readily and led the party to the command
vehicle. Howe had been bandaged and was lying quite still; he
was breathing heavily and was unconscious. He was carried
off on the stretcher. On the way back in the ambulance he
died.

That this could have happened to someone as close to
myself as Howe came as a sobering shock. The reality of death
in battle had touched me for the first time. The incident
seemed to typify all the incalculable perversity of the
battlefield whereby abruptly and at random a human being is
struck down – always when one least expects it and usually the
individual who least deserves it.

Lee now decided it would be safer for us to walk to
battalion headquarters. We started off down the track; but it
was pitch-black and the tangle of vehicle tracks so bewildering that we were compelled to abandon the attempt and made
instead for Headquarter Company HQ, which was near
Brigade. We borrowed blankets and tried to snatch some
sleep. At dawn I was picked up by the motor transport officer
and driven across the valley to join the main battalion.

Battalion headquarters was behind a low rising bluff, which
gave complete shelter from the enemy. There were a few Bren
carriers about and a number of hastily dug slit trenches. The
men were moving around freely and brewing up. Close by
were several burnt-out tanks and vehicles. The blackened
barrel of a knocked-out German 88 millimetre gun dominated the area. Over the top of the ridge in front, enemy
shells were bursting and banging. That was the salient in
which the battalion had spent the past forty-eight hours
under continuous mortar and shell-fire. Overnight the troops
had been withdrawn and the rifle companies were now dug in
along the reverse slope of the ridge.

I sat down on my valise feeling desolate, and thought how
comforting it must be to go into battle with people one knew.

What a consolation it would have been to set eyes on even one familiar face! The captain commanding the carrier platoon strolled over. His name was Jelley. He was young, with a clean appearance and a cool, self-possessed manner. He offered me a share of his breakfast and his batman handed over a plate of stew. I was dying to talk to someone, but after a few words he turned away and ignored me. I studied him. He was confident and composed, rather a stereotype of the English public schoolboy at war. He had spoken his few abrupt banalities with a certain hauteur, and he seemed quite unmoved by the events around him. As I later found out, he was in fact an officer of exceptional courage, but he seemed so natural and normal then that I assumed everyone in the battalion would be the same. This was a salutary encounter for me. I would have been mortified to have shown even the slightest sign of fear in his company.

A jeep drew up, and a smallish man with a moustache, shorts and a steel helmet jumped out. I took no notice until someone nudged me and whispered, 'The commanding officer.' I straightened myself up and said, 'Good morning, sir.' He addressed a few words to me and I explained why I had come. He was clearly in a hurry but after a moment's pause he remarked to his companion, 'We'll send him to Halsall in "B" Company,' adding as he turned back to me, 'I'm just on my way round there now. Hop in the jeep.' We drove across to 'B' Company headquarters, which was about six hundred yards to the right. The company commander was away making a reconnaissance, so I was entrusted to the reserve platoon nearby. As the colonel's jeep arrived a lieutenant stepped out of his trench, reluctantly it seemed to me, and saluted. The colonel introduced us briefly and drove off. 'Better get into the trench,' said the officer, for I was showing a disposition to stand and gossip in the early morning sunshine.

The trench was narrow, about four feet deep and five feet long. There was precious little room for the three of us, the officer, his sergeant and myself. No sooner had we taken cover than a shell burst in front, smothering us in a sea of loose sand. 'That was a near one,' said the sergeant. It all felt strangely unreal, like a scene from a second-rate film. We waited, but there were no more shells. The officer seemed swamped and overwhelmed by the strain of the battle. He turned to the sergeant. 'I suppose he had better take over Corporal Johnson's platoon.' The sergeant agreed. 'There it is, Ten Platoon,' he said, indicating a group of trenches about a hundred yards to the left.

6

I ran across to the platoon position. There were some seven or eight shallow slit trenches dug in the ground, ridiculously close together with scarcely a yard between them. The men, crouching in pairs in the shallow pits, looked lifeless and dispirited, and eyed me with some suspicion as I approached. The corporal seemed terribly young; he was a slender boy with fair hair falling down below his steel helmet and over his eyes. He was brighter-eyed and more awake than the others. 'I've come to take over the platoon,' I ventured, hoping not to appear intrusive. I need not have worried, for he made no attempt to conceal his delight. 'There's an empty trench, in the middle, sir,' he said pointing.

I climbed in and peeled off my pack and revolver belt. The corporal was beside me in a moment. 'You'd better have the glasses and compass, sir,' he said, divesting himself of these articles and handing them over. This gesture was to him a ritual act, the welcome renunciation of a disagreeable responsibility. There was something touching in his unconcealed relief. 'Are you the only NCO?' I asked. 'There's Lance-Corporal Bridgeman as well, sir. He's out looking for food for the boys.'

I scanned the surrounding area. This had been disputed territory a night or two before. Dotted plentifully about were the battered hulks of knocked-out vehicles and tanks, their blackened shapes poised at strange angles as though petrified by the shock of impact. From some oozed the sweet, sickly scent of scorched human flesh. A few corpses lay sprawled on the sand. The stiff unwanted bodies had a gruesome sameness with their heavy boots, steel helmets which pulled their heads down into the sand, and haversacks that kept their shoulders unnaturally taut. There was no comfort for them even in death as they lay there reeking and repulsive under the cruel sun.

Lance-Corporal Bridgeman came back. He was a gruff-voiced, sturdy yeoman, big and handsome, with an open, bronzed face and a broad Sussex accent. He brought some biscuits; they were charred, pitiful remnants, salvaged from a burnt-out tank. He handed them round. 'There's plenty more in the tank,' he said. The men were starving. 'We've had nothing since the attack,' they explained. I remembered that I had seen rations arriving at the same time as I had joined the company, so I ran over to company headquarters. Sure enough, there they were, being divided into platoon bundles and tied up in sacks. I grabbed ours and hurried back.

'But there's no water, sir!' It was lucky that I was bursting with energy after a good night's sleep and an ample breakfast. I thanked God for giving me something to do at last. This was what I was meant for. After the last two months of shiftless vagrancy I had at last found a home and a purpose. There were only two ways of getting water in the desert: to beg for it, or steal it. I was not particular which. I told Corporal Bridgeman to follow me and headed for battalion headquarters where there were some vehicles and the possibility of supplies.

I tackled a Scottish sergeant, who was standing beside his Bren gun carrier. There was something maddening about men who travelled into battle in vehicles. They always had their blankets, their overcoats, their rations and their water cans to hand; they didn't really know what war was like. 'My men have had no water for two days,' I explained. 'They're in a bad way. Can you let me have a couple of cans?' The sergeant eyed me distrustfully at first, but then he relaxed and produced three cans. The earnest face of the corporal might have persuaded him, or perhaps he saw a threatening look in my eye. For I am sure that if he had refused I would have knocked him to the ground and set fire to his vehicle.

Bridgeman and I ran back triumphantly to the platoon. The men were delighted, but were almost afraid to touch the water, it was so precious. 'Everyone will have half a mugful now. The rest will be kept for tea,' I announced with an authority and conviction that surprised me as much as it appeared to please the men.

I thought it wise before letting them start a fire to pay another quick call to company headquarters. I found the company commander, Captain John Halsall, sitting in his trench. He had returned from his reconnaissance. He was a short, red-headed Yorkshireman, who before the war had worked as a solicitor in Sussex. His hands and legs were swathed in dirty bandages, for he was suffering from those intolerable desert sores that never seemed to heal. Yet he sat there stoically, indifferent to his discomfort. I asked whether he would have any objection to my cooking a meal for the men. No, he answered, provided I included company headquarters, which was too small to cook for itself.

I doubled back and we picked the deepest trench of all. Two men came forward – they were the platoon cooks, they said, so I left them to it. They had scrounged a brew-can and some petrol from a derelict vehicle, and soon a fire was blazing. The meal was to be bully-beef stew, tea and biscuits. The rest of the men looked on, peering over the edges of their slit trenches with ravenous faces. The food was ready in about half an hour, when Corporal Bridgeman called out a gruff, 'Come and get it!' I watched the men scrambling out expectantly in ones and twos with their mess tins. Although it was quiet now, they seemed reluctant to leave the security of their trenches and did not waste a second getting back again. The meal was voted a tremendous success.

In the afternoon we were ordered to move across to the right – a matter of eight hundred yards or so. The battalion was to take over the positions occupied by the 2nd Battalion, who were being pulled back into reserve to refit for an attack the following night. We put on our equipment as darkness fell. We covered the ground quickly and there was no shelling; but an isolated enemy sniper was firing away in front. The rifle had a loud, elephantine report that was particularly startling. Though no bullets seemed to come near us, there was something vicious and treacherous in the noise, making us all feel uncomfortable. This was very different from the battle schools where machine guns rattled away all day within inches of you and grenades burst all around, yet you trotted through unharmed and contemptuous. Today, in the fading light, a single sniper kept a whole army on tenterhooks.

Our new platoon position was a distinct improvement on the old. It consisted of a group of captured German trenches, each large enough to hold a section of troops, and linked by a narrow communication trench. There was a deep, roomy security about these well-prepared and reinforced positions, and the men quickly settled in. One leg of the communication trench ran right up to the crest of the ridge in front and ended in a sizeable pit facing the enemy lines. This would make an ideal observation post, giving us in daylight a panorama of the battlefield. For the moment, however, nothing lay ahead but darkness and a deathly silence.

The men badly needed sleep and I decided they should stay in the deep slits to the rear, with just one sentry in the observation post at the head of the trench. We would all take it in turns to keep watch. The night was black and moonless, and the sentry would be on his own about thirty yards from the rest of the platoon. When I told the men what was wanted they nodded and moved away, but two of them came trailing back. Like all the rest they were worn out. One was a short, stocky man, with a dark wrinkled face and frightened, anxious eyes; the other was tall, thin, fair-haired and nervous-looking. They came up together and sheepishly said that they couldn't do it; they couldn't go into that forward position at night. I was rather taken aback, but I could see that they were quite in earnest. I told them they would have to do it. But they still insisted that it was impossible. I tried to look stern, but could hardly restrain a smile. This was an occasion when I was supposed to be ruthless, the moment when, according to convention, I should draw my revolver and drive them up at pistol point. Yet somehow I felt no resentment towards these men, only pity and understanding. After all it was essentially a personal matter. I carried my blanket and equipment into the observation post taking the two men with me and settled down there myself to sleep.

There was not much rest, though, that night. Out of the darkness we could hear the faint clinking of enemy mine-laying parties and the creaking whirr of moving tanks. To the north a tremendous barrage was rumbling. The guns behind were flashing from end to end of the horizon and the shells were landing away to the north, almost behind us, as the Australian Division attacked near the coast. But we were quite indifferent to this activity. To us nothing existed except our own sector; the rest was no more real than a canvas backcloth. Our interests were uniquely concentrated on the threatening strip of no man's land immediately facing us.

Though there was no action in our sector the enemy was

alert and sporadic bursts of fire came streaking over our lines. From a strongpoint in front an aggressive machine gun kept sending white streams of tracer, like thin cascades of shooting stars, over the battlefield. From right and left in our lines the Brens with their dogged staccato would pepper the enemy position; but whenever they fired there would be a swift and accurate response from the German gun. This arrogant Spandau dominated the battlefield with a brilliant and lordly defiance. Not to be outdone I borrowed a Bren and let loose a magazine. Back came the answer – a singing shower of bullets, whipping overhead and flickering out behind like tiny meteors.

In the morning we were up early. A blazing sun which had risen behind us was blinding the enemy. We were able to move freely along the communication trench and scrutinise the desert in safety from the parapet of the observation post. Less than a mile away on the skyline another long ridge ran parallel with our own. In between lay a broad expanse of soft sand, interspersed with one or two bare-looking mounds and patches of sparse, scrubby grass. This ground was occupied by the enemy – Italian troops mainly, but with a sprinkling of German infantry manning the strongpoints.

The nearest enemy position was about three or four hundred yards away, and with binoculars we could pick out here and there the tell-tale shadow of a narrow slit trench. The men engaged in casual sniping, but there was no reaction from the enemy. The whole scene seemed uncannily lifeless and deserted. It was difficult to visualise in those trenches the same sorts of activity as in ours and to credit that behind, over the ridge, were massed the teeming vehicles of another army. Occasionally I caught a glimpse of a figure stealing from one trench to the other. Then I would grab the German rifle I had acquired in place of my perfectly useless .38 revolver and blaze away across the sand. It was the expected thing to do, though I doubt if I ever hit anyone.

About ten yards in front of our observation post stood a battered Ford truck. I sprinted forward and crouched behind it to get a better view of the enemy positions. As I peered through the still morning air there was a splatter against the metal beside me. I was incredulous. There was a second smack, even closer. No mistake this time! I dropped to the ground and burrowed into the sand. But it was impossible to feel scared on such a beautiful morning. I was embarrassed rather than frightened, though I began to miss the deep security of the trench behind. I considered making a dash for it but remembered the instructions that snipers were given. The secret, they were always taught, was concentration. The sniper should wait patiently for his prey, his eye glued to the sights, for five minutes, even a quarter of an hour, if necessary. I pictured a conscientious Hun, his rifle trained painstakingly on the gap and I judged it inexpedient to put his marksmanship to the test.

Bridgeman had heard the firing and crawled into the observation post to try to help. After about five minutes I decided to chance it. I made it back to the post in a couple of seconds. No shot was fired. It was a disappointment in a way, and rather belied the current concept of Teutonic infallibility.

In the shelter of the platoon positions the two cooks, Duke and Pett, were busy preparing another meal. Everyone else was foraging in the slits, savouring for the first time the unparalleled joys of looting. The position was littered with abandoned German kit – clothing, arms and ammunition. A few quick changes of underclothes were effected; some men donned jackboots; others probed into the meticulously written diaries which were scattered around, and the colourful magazines. We all played with the smart Afrika Korps caps and the novel steel helmets and respirators. The first impromptu encounter with enemy equipment always had a great fascination.

We enjoyed a good breakfast, being careful to leave sufficient for another meal later. But a message came that we were to collect more rations from company headquarters. Two men returned with an incredible burden of tins and water cans, the accumulated rations of at least three days. A hasty plebiscite revealed that the men were in favour of another meal at once; so the cooks set to work. We had just sat back replete when the colour-sergeant arrived with a cooked meal from the rear echelon. He had been keeping it hot in containers for two days, but had not been allowed to bring it forward. At first I thought of refusing this meal but the men, with their superior wisdom, would not hear of it. As they settled down to eat once more, I marvelled at the insatiable appetite of the private soldier.

In the trench it was warm and comfortable. There was spasmodic shelling, but the deep, narrow slits offered complete protection. Our anxieties were temporarily lulled. It was an acceptable, interesting experience. I was surprised how rapidly one became used to these surroundings, to the grisly company of the shattered tanks and the fly-blown corpses. I was surprised, too, by the way I came to know each of the men individually in the space of twenty-four hours. Not only had I learned all their names but I could judge exactly what each man was worth and what each would be capable of in battle. At such close quarters one could see into their very souls.

Most of the men became quite perky in the course of the day. I had arrived without a steel helmet and my soft cap was a matter of concern to them. One of them offered to get me a helmet. He returned a little later with an excellent one, although the peculiar, sickly fragrance left little doubt as to the fate of the previous owner. Another man, Cross, came up and in a burst of embarrassment confided that he had been batman to the previous officer, wounded the night before I arrived. Could he look after me? 'I don't quite see what there is for you to do,' I said, 'but I should only be too pleased to have you.' Henceforward I had the services of a gentleman's gentleman, although the circumstances made the office something of a sinecure.

As the sun rose higher the battlefield began to come to life. There was more shelling on both sides and some machine-gun fire. A sniper made us keep our heads down, and to move about we had to crawl on all fours along the communication trench. Although it afforded some protection there was one snag: it had been in intermittent use as a latrine. Only a few of the more intrepid and fastidious members of the platoon adopted the technique of the 'horizontal rear', which was performed lying on one's side by the edge of the trench, with one eye on the enemy and a hand balancing behind on the parapet – an uncomfortable and hazardous proceeding.

An enemy machine gun was active in front, firing in savage bursts. The intervening ridge protected us and the bullets sailed harmlessly over the top. They struck the ground behind, near battalion headquarters; there, fat and un-athletic figures went to ground with surprising agility. This edifying spectacle gave the men a profound, if unethical,

El Alamein: the battlefield.

Examining captured enemy documents at 133 Brigade HQ.
The author is on the extreme right.

Burnt-out German tracked motorcycle.

Early prisoners taken by soldiers of the Royal Sussex Regiment.

satisfaction. One of them expressed the hope that the bullets were landing round the regimental sergeant-major's trench. Not that he had anything against that individual but here, as in any unit, the RSM personified all that the private soldier most detested about the army.

The novelty and excitement of the surrounding activity gave us, in the relative security of our own position, a sense of exhilaration. In the afternoon I thought I would wander over to the company commander for a chat. When I reached the trench I found he was not there. 'Where's Captain Halsall?' I asked. The signaller looked up. 'He's gone to battalion headquarters, sir, to get the orders for an attack.' The words struck a chill in my stomach. That was how fear could hit you. It was evoked by sudden associations: by the grating burst of an isolated shell; by the sniff of cordite in a wrecked vehicle; by the sudden sight of a pale, stiff corpse; or by those unwelcome words 'orders for an attack'.

I decided to wait for the company commander, and later the two other platoon commanders, Sergeant Homden and Sergeant White, joined me. When Halsall came back he squatted in the trench and slowly opened his notebook. He seemed abnormally calm. The rest of us did our best to simulate unconcern but the atmosphere was tense and the anxiety showed in people's eyes. It was infuriating the way the company commander checked everyone present and read through his notes carefully before starting.

'The New Zealanders are attacking tonight with the biggest barrage of the battle since the bombardment on the opening night,' he began. 'They are going in north of this position, and the 2nd Battalion will be alongside them. We shall be following behind the 2nd and then our job is to pinch off a little sector to the south to make the salient more secure. The route westwards from the start line will be marked with tapes. At the end of the tape we shall turn south on a compass bearing for a thousand paces to our objective. One man in each platoon will keep count.' It sounded modest and innocent enough. How much better it always was when one knew the details.

I walked across to the platoon. They were all waiting. I was conscious of their grim, concentrated scrutiny. Unwittingly I was caught up in the masquerade. The roles were reversed and now they would find exasperation in my calm. I collected everyone together in the deepest pit and drew a diagram in the sand with my stick. As I began to brief them, I was suddenly very conscious of their individuality and of each man's burning desire to live.

We were all afraid now. Before an attack fear is universal. The popular belief that in battle there are two kinds of person – the sensitive, who suffer torment, and the unimaginative few who know no fear and go blithely on – is a fallacy. Everyone was as scared as the next man, for no imagination was needed to foresee the possibility of death or mutilation. It was just that some managed to conceal their fear better than others. Officers could not afford to show their feelings as openly as the men; they had more need to dissemble. In a big battle a subaltern had little or no influence over the fate of his platoon – it was the plaything of the gods. His role was essentially histrionic. He had to feign a casual and cheerful optimism to create an illusion of normality and make it seem as if there was nothing in the least strange about the outrageous things one was asked to do. Only in this way could he ease the tension, quell any panic and convince his men that everything would come out right in the end.

Inwardly I marvelled that they did not take to their heels. They grumbled and looked apprehensive, but nothing more. Why, I asked myself, do men not run away in battle? They are held back by the thread of self-respect, by a refusal to be shamed in front of their comrades. Courage is essentially competitive and imitative. Everyone is susceptible to leadership, and example is what counts. I could see that Halsall was going to do what he said he would. I was determined to do anything he could do. Johnson and Bridgeman thought, 'If an officer can do it, we damn well can.' The men looked to the NCOs and said to themselves, 'We'll go wherever the bloody corporals go.' Thus an army stands firm.

I gave them all the encouragement I could, assuring them the opposition would be slight, perhaps non-existent. There would be nothing to it really. They looked immensely relieved. They had a touching faith in anything an officer told them. Then it was time for sterner stuff and I ended on a cruel note: 'In the last attack I am told that several men fell behind under the pretext of helping their wounded friends. This must not happen tonight. The wounded are to be left on the ground. The stretcher-bearers will pick them up. If anyone is late reaching the objective, he will be treated as a deserter.' I frowned and looked severe though I didn't mean a word of it. I told them to break away and clean their weapons. I primed two grenades and stuffed one into each pocket of my shorts. The colour-sergeant supplied extra shovels for the platoon – one between two men – and empty sandbags which we tucked in our haversacks, together with a battle ration of one tin of bully beef and a packet of hard biscuits. My mind was full of urgent practical problems

Late in the afternoon a company from the Highland Division arrived to take over our sector. They came up in scattered sections, each moving into its allotted position. Although the light was fading the Germans spotted them and bombarded us with air-burst shells.

The reports seemed to come from just over the ridge in front, each one followed by a fiendish roar and an ugly red flash. The shrapnel fragments exploded around us before biting into the sand. The weapons seemed to be searching their way all along the front. A section of Jocks doubled the last few hundred yards and leapt into our trench. The explosions came nearer, rocking the ground and showering us with sand. We crouched down, tense and silent. But the noise passed. It was all over and there were no casualties.

The trench was now uncomfortably overcrowded. But there was security in numbers and the Scots had brought food in containers, which they insisted on sharing with us. The platoon commander pressed me to take some. It was a frugal meal – tepid stew and biscuit pudding – and I had little appetite, but I accepted it out of politeness. In the middle of the meal a Jock came stumbling into the trench asking to see the officer. He wanted to make a complaint about the food. He was a sullen specimen, with a confused and husky Scots voice. 'What's the matter with the food?' he was asked. 'It's cold and there's no' enough of it,' he mumbled. The officer laughed at him and told him to 'bugger off'. He slouched away cursing. The complaint – in the forward salient on the eve of an attack – was a ridiculous one. Yet there was a certain ring of defiance about it. When the Day of Judgement comes, the British soldier will vanish into the ultimate chaos with a complaint about the food on his lips.

The officer and I got on splendidly together. He seemed a

bit aloof at first, with a certain English reserve although he was in a Scots regiment. But we warmed to each other rapidly. We talked dispassionately about the forthcoming attack. We knew the implications well enough, but stuck to practicalities. 'You must keep dispersed,' he advised me. 'On the first night we only lost three men. "A" Company, who bunched up, lost a good many more. Oh, it's not so bad, once you get going.' We chatted for about an hour on a variety of topics and found we understood each other perfectly. Then he curled up in the trench and went to sleep.

The moon had not yet risen, but the desert was bathed in wan starlight and the night was chilly. I only had a battledress top over my shirt and shorts and I couldn't stop shivering. We were not to move off until midnight and there were still a couple of hours to go, with nothing to do but sit and wait. Waiting, waiting, waiting. The uncertainty was unbearable. Now I had no one to talk to, I was oppressed with a dread of the future. For the first time I felt nervous, a peculiar gnawing restlessness, a vague uneasiness, an emptiness of the stomach, a desire to be anywhere but here at this moment. Yet true fear should be something more, I thought – an overwhelming sensation of terror and paralysis; this was slight, but hauntingly persistent. It would have been negligible if only one could have put an end to the intolerable suspense.

Life was now free of all its complexities. What a clarity and a simplicity it really had! To stay alive, to lead once more a normal existence, to know again warmth, comfort and safety – what else could one conceivably demand? I would never chide circumstance again, never question fate, never feel bored, unhappy or dissatisfied. That would be unthinkable. To be allowed to continue to live – nothing else mattered. I clenched my fists, closed my eyes and prayed to God that I might survive. Eventually I fell into a fitful sleep.

7

A shout from the company commander awakened me from my doze. It was past midnight, the time when we were due to move off. Dashing frantically round the trenches, I roused the men and hurried them on with their equipment. Fear quite vanished in this burst of activity. Within a few moments we joined the remainder of the company and began to march back to battalion headquarters where the rest of the unit had already assembled. There was hardly a sound, except for some coughing from the rows of restless men making their final preparations for the advance. When the signal was given we set off northwards, one company at a time. In a shadowy procession the columns marched calmly and quickly into the darkness.

I could scarcely believe this was a real night attack. It was just like an exercise; the routine was so familiar. Yet there was a difference – for there were no umpires and we took liberties which would never have passed in training. The men tramped along in threes, pressing so close behind each other that there was not an inch of space between them, all but the first file fortified by the questionable belief that a shell splinter might hit the front man but those behind would be safe. Every platoon seemed to be squeezed up like this. The officers did not object, for it kept the troops together and was the only certain way to avoid losing anyone. In war, if you wanted to chance something, you did so and took the consequences. So we marched bunched together and to Hell with the rules!

Now the cumbersome column turned west towards the enemy. We were halted on the top of a bald mound, which was to be the forming-up point. We were too early. The approach march had been easier and quicker than expected and we had the best part of half an hour to wait. The sand seemed as hard as stone as we strove vainly to scoop shallow slits for our protection. We couldn't have picked a worse spot, but at least it was quiet. From here we were to advance in column before turning south in an extended line into the attack. We lay down in the sand and waited.

Then the barrage began. From a long way to the rear came the smacking roar of the 25-pounders, merging into a continuous rumble, like a hundred gigantic muffled typewriters. The sky was lit with a red, unearthly glow. There was a moment's pause before the shells sped overhead in clusters like swarms of angry bees. They were so low that you felt you could reach up and touch them as they raced thicker and faster after each other until they fell, ripping up the sand along our front. The Bofors with their stark, ear-splitting crack sprayed long bursts of fiery tracers down the flanks. A whole battalion of heavy Vickers machine guns began firing right alongside us, raking the enemy lines and adding their heavy, saturating chatter to the general din. Altogether it was the most unholy row I had ever heard in my life. We were dazed and bewildered, and did not notice that the company in front had begun to move. We spotted them at the last moment and started up, dashing after them.

How minute and fragile one felt, trapped in this maelstrom of explosive fury! When we moved forward we scuttled like mice across the inhospitable sand in flexible little groups, ready to sway and flatten ourselves to earth if a shell burst nearby. Without warning we stumbled on the company in front once again. Another prolonged incomprehensible halt! The enemy shelling had blown away the tape leading to the start line and the battalion intelligence officer, Lieutenant Cairncross, who was directing the column, had been wounded. There were several minutes of delay and general disorder while the leaders reorientated themselves.

The enemy mortars were retaliating and a few ominous flashes appeared among the ranks of 'A' Company ahead. There was some confused shouting from the front. We dropped to our knees and dug for all we were worth. An enemy Spandau flickered up out of the darkness, its pert, swift, 'grr. . .p' unmistakable above the thunder of the barrage, and sent sharp streams of tracer hissing past into the blackness of the night. We were being fired upon. Though this was the very meaning of war, I felt a sense of outrage and betrayal. Someone had blundered. We were some reckless, sacrificial offering to the vanity of the divisional commander. The attack would fail and we would be massacred. How could this chaos conceivably resolve itself into a successful attack? Yet all the major battles of history must have seemed like this, a hopeless shambles to the individual in front, with a coherence only discernible to those in the rear.

A runner appeared. 'Follow me, sir,' he shouted. I set off after him, the platoon closing up behind. 'A' Company had vanished, but soon the sturdy figure of Halsall loomed through the darkness in front. 'This is where we turn south – a thousand paces and dig in,' he shouted, pointing the way. He was struggling to make himself heard above the din. At last we had clear and positive instructions. It was almost a pleasure to move into the attack. Anything to get off that dreadful bare mound! The platoon deployed quickly and we charged forward through the dark, swirling sand across the smoking shell holes reeking with cordite.

By bad luck we collided with the tail of the 2nd Battalion, which was advancing at right angles to us. More shouts, more confusion, more delay. But we sorted ourselves out and pressed on, eager to complete our thousand paces; one man was counting aloud beside me. Three Germans suddenly emerged from the smoky screen, hands above their heads. Drab, cringing creatures they were, looking drawn and terrified. There was no time to bother with them, just a quick curse as we rushed past. Next we came upon some slit trenches. Somebody inside refused to budge, so one of the men put a bullet in. To our horror it proved to be an isolated outpost on the extreme edge of a Scottish position. An officer stormed up, a tall, wild-eyed Highlander. He was furious. He singled me out and began kicking up a hell of a row. It was very regrettable, but I hadn't time to attend to him. I told him to 'belt up' and pushed ahead.

We plunged once more into the cloud of sand and smoke. We had nearly covered the distance and there appeared to be no more Germans. The earlier information must have been right after all. Damned good staff at Division! We reached another slight incline in the sand with a tufted, scrubby fringe and the company commander shouted, 'Dig in!' The men had already slung their rifles in anticipation and their shovels were to the fore. They set to with a will.

Bewildering explosions and alarming flashes continued all around us – but they held less terror now. From time to time an 88mm thundered out in front and with a terrific roar the shot went wailing over our heads. As often as not the shell found its mark and a vehicle went up in flames. The enemy mortars, too, were busy, but mostly they over-shot our position and we heard the dull crumps at the rear. We were on our knees absorbed in digging and oblivious to everything else. The sand was so soft that as fast as we dug the sides came tumbling in again and we had to use sandbags to buttress them. Cross and I took it in turns with the shovel in our joint trench. When we had finished I walked across to 'A' Company to make contact with the flanking platoon, and on the way back called to report at our own company headquarters.

Halsall was helping the signallers dig a trench. 'We have to make it deep because of the wireless,' he remarked, half apologetically.

There was a lot of solid, un-selfconscious heroism in John Halsall. No dramatics, but an air of quiet resolution, a perceptible determination to carry out whatever task he was given. When issuing instructions for the attack to platoon commanders he had explained that he would not himself be marching in front. 'The CO has given orders that company headquarters must be kept in the rear.' Nevertheless, within a few moments of the start he was up in front with his runner, in the thick of it. Now he stood, spade in hand, untidy bandages covering the desert sores on his hands and legs and ginger hair sticking out in tufts under his steel helmet, blinking through his spectacles, diffident but unshakable.

I strolled back the hundred yards towards the platoon but they had disappeared. I combed the area but there was no trace of them. Feeling foolish and panicking hopelessly, I went back to the company commander and told him the horrible truth. He joined me in the hunt. We wandered round absurdly in all directions calling out 'Ten Platoon!'; but there was no response. It was a ludicrous situation. At last we heard a grunt, and noticed a handful of shallow slit trenches looking like shadows in the sand. No matter that the enemy were only a few hundred yards away, the men had lain down and gone to sleep. I shook them awake, cursed them and ordered them to dig a foot deeper and bury their loose equipment in the sand, for it was lying higgledy-piggledy around the trenches. Dawn could not be far off.

The platoon dug in pairs. That was always the way, each man sharing with his mate. It was curious this rugged intimacy that sprang up between men in battle – the inseparability of mates. They would live, eat, work and sleep together and could not bear to be parted. If one of them was killed or wounded the other was quite lost. 'Mac' had lost his mate in this way, and now he was jittery and demoralised. Bridgeman said, 'Mac'll be all right. I'll have him in with me for a couple of days.' So a new partnership came about.

When the trenches seemed deep enough, I posted a sentry and told the rest of the men to go to sleep. I intended to keep awake but it was an unequal struggle. After nodding for a while I too dropped off. When I awoke it was broad daylight and I was amazed to see how close all the trenches in the platoon were to one another. To the left Twelve Platoon were stirring in their slits. 'A' Company was on the right, but there was an alarming gap between us. In front the tell-tale outline of an enemy position was visible among the burnt-out husks of scattered vehicles.

Cross and I shared a narrow trench about five feet long, two feet wide and two feet deep. We lay with our heads at opposite ends in superb discomfort. It was impossible to stretch at full length. Our knees stuck into each other, and we had to twist our heads sideways to keep them below the top of the slit. What was more, I had to accommodate a case with two sticky bombs in the trench – the sole anti-tank defence of the platoon – which I clung to for psychological rather than material protection. It was breakfast time and we opened a tin of bully beef. We had no knives, and we took it in turns to dip our fingers in, for the beef had become a soft pliable mess in the heat. We spread it on some dry biscuits, washing it down with a swig of water from the bottle.

To the front, between 'A' Company and ourselves, was a large dark patch of scrub. From the middle of this a white flag suddenly fluttered. A couple of shabby enemy soldiers appeared from below ground. Soon there were a dozen of them hesitantly standing with their hands above their heads. They came slowly forward. What a tantalising moment it must have been for them poised on the verge of no man's land. All along our lines heads popped up above the slit trenches in wonderment and jubilation. A tiny, slippery Italian with an enormous white banner zigzagged in front. He had a humble, over-eager smile on his face, though he flinched perceptibly every time he heard an explosion. As the others drew closer and realised that we were not going to fire on them they quickened their pace. A couple of men from 'A' Company ran out and after a quick search hustled them back to battalion headquarters.

Meanwhile, we could hear from behind the noise of moving armour; our tanks were trying to percolate through the corridor occupied by the infantry. Occasionally a tank would climb over the ridge and ease slowly westward across the desert. There would be a flash and a roar from the enemy 88mm in the strongpoint ahead of us, and chunks of metal would fly off in all directions. After a first slow crackle of flame, the tank would begin to brew up fiercely in the distance. It was depressing to see the armour making so little progress and we lay in our slit trenches with our heads down throughout the morning.

Towards noon the commanding officer called an 'order group' at battalion headquarters. Halsall and I were both summoned. We ran back across the open ground together. Colonel McCully was in good spirits and there was a breezy informality about the group. 'How did you enjoy last night?' he asked me. 'Oh, all right, sir,' I answered, 'but there was a hell of a lot of noise.' 'That's right,' he said. 'It's nearly all noise . . . I've got a little job for you tonight.' He pointed to the charred shell of a tank near the enemy strongpoint. 'I want you to attack that position with your platoon. Personally I don't think you'll find anyone there – but it might be fun to blow up the tank.' 'Yes, sir,' I replied, as one did in such circumstances, and went back to the platoon to think it out.

I was sceptical about the colonel's assessment. Corporal Johnson, with the aid of my binoculars, had spotted phantom Germans flitting in and out all morning. There was always something distasteful, too, about a small-scale raid; it seemed such a senseless waste from the individual's point of view. Later, I was pondering on the task ahead when I noticed the company commander beckoning to me from his headquarters. I went over and he told me, 'Your raid is cancelled tonight. It's going to be a battalion attack instead. We go in at last light. There will be hot cocoa and rum on the objective. Later tonight we shall be relieved by the Black Watch and pulled back into reserve.' No attack is welcome, but this one certainly offered its compensations.

In the late afternoon a battalion of the Seaforths launched an attack to our right. We were not expecting it but to our delight the entire unit in perfect formation appeared unheralded from behind and marched steadily through 'A' Company's lines towards the enemy. They were supported by tanks which nosed, crab-like, around the flank and drenched the enemy strongpoint with small-arms fire. An intrepid armoured car, filtering to the left, began a duel with the 88mm, which was the pivot of the enemy defences. For the first time the 88 had the worst of it. It fired several shots in exchange but they fell wide of the mark. Then our gunners brought their fire right on top of it. They must have scored a direct hit, for the 88 fell silent. Our battalion mortars were also active, laying a screen of smoke in front of the enemy trenches.

Meanwhile, the infantry were moving slowly and relentlessly forward in text-book order. The weight of the attack was well to our right, though the men on the extreme left skirted our position as they passed. No sight could have been more comforting. There was something immensely solid and resolute about these troops as they advanced in neatly deployed groups with their bayonets fixed. When the leading sections had penetrated about a thousand yards they began to dig in. Unexpectedly, from the scrub directly in front of us, about thirty more Italians rose up and came forward to give themselves up. The carefully camouflaged trenches were much closer than we had ever suspected, and the occupants had contrived to remain completely out of sight throughout the day. Corporal Johnson and a couple of men ran out to search them.

Surprisingly, I could feel no hostility towards these Italians. Rather I was disposed to compliment them on their good sense in surrendering when they did, for if we had had to fight them half of us could have been killed. They aroused my curiosity, though. Prisoners are most intriguing at the first moment of capture, when their faces register a blend of shame, bewilderment and suspicion. How vulnerable these men looked in their predicament. I longed to talk to them, to find out what they made of it all. There is a singular fellowship amongst infantrymen, for whichever side they fight. Their lives run closely parallel in the face of a common undiscriminating slaughter. But there was no time for conversation. After we had disarmed the prisoners and sent them to the rear we sat in our slits waiting for the order to advance.

To dispel any false sense of security on our part an enemy mortar opened fire. One bomb burst near company headquarters and another fell quite close to us. Cross and I cowered in the trench and waited until the bombing ceased. When I cautiously poked my head up I heard a startled shout from the neighbouring trench, 'Man hit here, sir.' I rushed over. Corporal Johnson was sitting upright in his slit trench and moaning slightly. He must have kept his head and shoulders above ground to watch the bursting bomb. A red stain was oozing through his left breast-pocket. Rose, the platoon stretcher-bearer, arrived and began cutting open his shirt with his scissors to dress the wound. Suddenly he looked up, horrified. The corporal's body had stiffened, his eyes were fixed and vacant: he was dead.

For my part, I felt no revulsion or horror. I almost rebuked myself for my insensibility. But this termination of one human life made no difference to the rest of us. In action there was no time for death; it was merely an ugly inconvenience. There was no pathos either. Nerves were too taut and reactions too disciplined for those involved to feel ordinary human emotions. Death is touching only when it can be related to the normal pattern of life. When one can visualise a man at home with his family, only then can the tragic brutality of the sacrifice be appreciated. In battle one was blind to this, and aware only of an instinctive and overwhelming sense of relief at the thought, 'Thank God it wasn't me!'

I glanced down in the trench and said to Rose, 'Leave *him* here – and you come with me.' 'I . . . come . . . with you.' He repeated the words mechanically, absentmindedly, glad to cling to the living and thankful to escape the dead thing beside him. The company commander was now waving us on. We slid out of our trenches and as darkness fell moved swiftly across the sand, carefully counting the paces. Cross and I were in the centre with a section on each side. We closed upon our objective. So far there was no opposition. Here on the rising ground were silhouetted two knocked-out tanks, which the Germans had converted into ammunition dumps. They were both on fire, blazing fiercely. The eerie crackling echoed across the desert; showers of sparkling lights were scattered in all directions and sinister shadows danced to and fro over the sand. From further on came the noise of vehicles starting up. The enemy seemed to be pulling out.

We lengthened our stride. At the foot of the low mound which had been the enemy's main position was a barbed-wire fence. We crawled through and advanced up the slope in an extended line There was a sudden roar beside me, an ear-splitting report and a wicked crimson flash. Mines! I was knocked headlong, my ears singing. I was not hurt, but I lay still for a moment. There were gasps and cries of pain from close beside me. Three men in the left-hand section had been hit, not ten yards away. One must have been blown to bits for we never found him again; another was sitting upright sobbing, holding his head and bleeding from the ears. The third man was writhing in the sand with his leg blown off. I sent what I could find of the platoon back to the foot of the mound to wait. The stretcher-bearer attended to the man with the missing leg and I looked to the other. He was still crying, but more from shock than injury it seemed to me. It was hopeless trying to help here, fumbling in the darkness and smothered in sand. Eventually I managed to run a couple of field dressings around his head. 'Will I be all right, sir?' he kept asking. 'Sure, sure, you're OK. Just sit quiet and you've got nothing to worry about.' I knelt beside him and put my arm around him to comfort him. A couple of stretcher-bearers arrived. The wounded man had been clutching my hand like a child and was reluctant to let go. Away he went at last, a little more cheerful now; but he died all the same an hour later in the ambulance.

A medical orderly came across from the other man, shaking his head. He whispered, 'No good, sir. I went to put a torniquet on his leg but when I felt for the stump I found that his whole buttock was blown away. I can't stop the bleeding. He'll be dead in a few moments.' We had no choice but to leave him where he was.

When I rejoined the platoon they had already been ordered to dig in. The sand was soft on top but firm underneath, and in no time at all we were a couple of feet below the surface, digging with a silent, nervous ferocity. Someone had called an artillery barrage down on the mound in front. The shells were skimming over our heads, tearing up the sand before us. It was a vicious barrage and much too close for comfort. Then magically it stopped and everything was quiet again. Tea was brought up in containers. This lukewarm, insipid brew was far short of the hot cocoa and rum we had been promised, but welcome nonetheless. One by one the men dropped off to sleep.

A field telephone had been connected to the company. The bell rang and I picked it up. 'Do you know where the CO is?' 'Yes, I have seen him go forward with the company commander.' 'Will you please take a message to him from the adjutant: the relief has *not* arrived yet at battalion headquarters.' 'Yes I'll tell him that.' I walked up the mound across the ghostly minefield to where four officers were standing in a group, the colonel, Halsall, Captain Richards – commanding

'A' Company – and a major from the Royal Engineers. Though fully exposed, they did not seem to show any concern. The enemy had evidently pulled out completely. I passed on the message and waited. Some sappers had cleared a narrow lane through the minefield and were marking the path with tape. After a few minutes the CO said that the battalion could now move forward up the slope. 'A' Company would advance first and deploy to the right at the top; 'B' Company would follow, deploying to the left.

We rejoined the men at the foot of the mound. After some coughing and rustling of equipment 'A' Company began to advance slowly in single file up the slope. In 'B' Company we stood ready in our slits waiting for them to get clear. The leading troops were half way up when, from about a hundred yards in front, there was the smack of a single Very light cartridge. It soared into the sky and burst over us at its peak, illuminating the area with a lingering flood of brilliance. 'A' Company were straggled in a line along the tape. The enemy must have reoccupied their positions on top of the mound. A Spandau opened up sending a hail of bullets into the middle of the company. Then there were sharp, single cracks of rifle-fire, sounding alarmingly loud and close. Two more white Very lights shot up and after a tantalising pause burst in a shower overhead. Caught in this pool of light some of the men fell flat on their faces; the rest stood like statues. They were hopelessly trapped. The ranks were raked by fire, and after a few moments the company turned and fled back to their slit trenches, dragging the wounded as best they could.

The rest of the battalion seemed momentarily paralysed. But then the Brens began chattering and the mortars in battalion headquarters opened up on the enemy. Halsall was yelling for me. 'The CO wants you to attack with your platoon on the left flank,' he said. It sounded a dubious business to me. I told him I would need more men than my depleted platoon. 'You'll have to take some of Eleven Platoon,' he replied. I dashed round trying to rouse them. They were remarkably unenthusiastic, those that were not half asleep. It was hell to get anything done with someone else's platoon. I told the sergeant, 'Wake your blokes up. They'll be needed for an attack in five minutes.' Meanwhile the enemy had stopped firing, and the mound was dark and silent once more.

I decided to reconnoitre with the handful of my own men I was able to muster immediately. These were Lance-Corporal Bridgeman, Henderson, Paddy Mahon and young Cobb. I had the best of them there, and we would do what we could. We edged forward on tip-toe, working round to the left. The battalion mortars were bombarding the enemy position, although some of the bombs were landing near us. I told the men to take cover behind a hump in the sand while Bridgeman and I crawled cautiously forward. We were getting close now. Mercifully it was pitch-dark. Another Very light and we would have been finished.

We could just make out the faint skyline of the enemy mound. Then we glimpsed a couple of shadowy silhouettes darting from trench to trench. A few hasty, guttural whispers carried across the sand. From further left came the clatter of picks and shovels; some of the party were digging fresh trenches. The Germans were clearly here in some strength. A couple of dozen, I reckoned. Bridgeman agreed. 'I was thinking, sir,' he murmured slowly, 'It's not going to be much use attacking that lot with only five of us.' My thoughts were the same. As we peered through the darkness one of the men crawled forward to join us and whispered, 'They're calling for us in the company, sir. We're to go back right away. We've been relieved.' The Black Watch had arrived.

We were still too close to take any chances. I sent the others back while Bridgeman covered them with the Bren gun. Then we followed. John Halsall, who was collecting the company together, greeted me warmly. 'Glad you're back, I thought you'd gone for good. The rendezvous is where we were this morning. We'll be picked up by transport and pulled out. Make your way independently as soon as Eleven Platoon is clear.'

The other platoon had already fitted on their equipment. As the first few men moved out of the trenches there was a sharp explosion – booby-traps! A shrapnel mine had spattered among them. There were frightened and bewildered cries from the wounded. Crack! That was another one. The company was in a turmoil. Above the din Halsall was thundering the hideous, blood-curdling call for stretcher-bearers. Oh God! How could this happen now of all times? But it was no good hanging about so I shouted to the platoon, 'Follow close behind me. I know the way out.' This was pure bluff, but the men flocked around me and with the courage of desperation we tramped out of the position and made our way back to rear battalion headquarters without mishap.

8

There was a mad scramble on the track leading back from the front, a general congestion of carriers, jeeps and marching troops. When I had put the platoon safely on the track I doubled back to the colonel to tell him about my reconnaissance. 'Better report that to the CO of the Black Watch,' he said. I retraced my steps until I found one of the Scottish officers. I let him know what I could about the enemy numbers and their dispositions, and he undertook to pass the information on. Then I hurried after the platoon. They had just left in trucks, I was told at the rendezvous. The anti-tank officer was there and he offered me a lift on a portée.

The grey light of dawn was spreading across the horizon as the vehicle bumped over the sand. About half-a-dozen of us were slumped in the back. Everyone was silent. It was the heavy, brooding silence of men who have just had a shattering experience, when the full impact strikes their consciousness for the first time. The driver went at full speed, racing to reach the rear before daylight could betray our movements and bring down a spate of shelling. We were parched, hungry and exhausted; our eyes smarted as we fought to hold off sleep. All the horror of the night came crowding into our minds. But as the portée drew closer and closer to safety we began to relax. This might be only a brief reprieve before an accumulation of worse horrors, but we clung to it thankfully all the same.

At rear echelon behind the minefield I spotted the company commander. The transport had been collected together – the cooks' trucks with their cookers blazing, troop carriers and even the company office truck. But there was no platoon. I must have overtaken them on the way back. However, there was a glut of water, and everyone seemed to be soaking themselves from cut-away petrol tins which were overflowing with hot, soapy suds. There never was such water! I stripped and rinsed my tired limbs from top to toe. Afterwards I helped myself to a plate of stew and a mug of tea, which for once was really piping hot. It was bliss to stretch out at full length across the open sand in complete safety. But there was still no platoon. I cursed myself for ever having left them.

By mid-morning they had still not appeared, and I decided to go back and search. Sergeant Brooks of the carrier platoon claimed to have seen them earlier at a 'stragglers' post', and I persuaded him to take me there in a spare troop carrier, which we commandeered. We drove across the main minefield through clouds of dust and along a welter of tracks. We spent the whole afternoon on a fruitless hunt; there was no sign of the platoon. We were forced to break off the search when night fell, but resolved to resume it at first light.

We were in the forward gun line, amid the flashes and deafening reports of the 25-pounders. We each found a slit trench; I huddled inside mine, knees doubled up, wrapped in a gritty blanket, using my haversack as a pillow. Sleep was almost impossible in that cold and smoky hole, with the guns booming all around. Fearsome, too, were the rumbling tanks that might at any moment lose the narrow track and come thundering over the top of the trench.

It was a relief when day broke and we were able to set off again on our search. An Indian division was deployed around us. The troops were brewing up, squatting and shivering around their miserable, crackling twig fires. Brooks and I scoured the area but without success. After a couple of hours we gave up and drove slowly back to the company. At the rear echelon – to my joy – I spotted the platoon. Apparently we had missed them by only a few minutes the previous afternoon.

I was too relieved to dwell on our wasted effort and hurried across to greet them. Paddy Mahon was the first to speak. 'We're getting back into the trucks, sir, and moving forward again – Jerry's on the run.' The enemy had been routed, and the division was concentrating for the pursuit battle. Yet, strangely, the news of our victory was in a sense a blow. What we needed was rest. Instead we would be caught up in the tumult of a successful offensive and hurled once more into the cauldron.

The men had recovered astonishingly quickly. Twenty-four hours ago I would have said they were finished. But now – after a meal, a wash and a night's sleep – they accepted the new development phlegmatically. 'Of course,' they seemed to be saying, 'we were promised a ten day's dog fight – and then a bus ride to Tripoli ... Well, this must be the bus ride.' They threw their equipment into the trucks and hauled themselves aboard.

The long, ponderous convoy moved off through the minefield, past the bare mound where we had crouched before the night attack and straight through the abandoned enemy positions. We swung to the right into a patch of softish sand. Here the company commanders were waiting. Halsall told us to dig in for all-round anti-tank defence. We were heartened to learn that several thousand prisoners had been taken that morning, including von Thoma, commander of the Afrika Korps. Later fresh orders arrived; we were to escort a petrol and oil column to Daba. The vehicles deployed in desert formation in readiness. Then a flight of Stukas pounced on us. For a few seconds there was pandemonium, with bombs dropping around us and bullets ripping up the sand. We leapt from the trucks and flung ourselves to the ground. A troop of Bofors guns sprang into action; the teams were in the open pelting shells into the air. Behind us a truck was hit and burst into flames. Luckily the raiders soon passed and the sky was empty again.

We continued on our way but did not get very far before being halted at a spot where a line of telegraph poles ran obliquely across the desert. We stayed there all afternoon and at nightfall dug in and posted sentries; away to the front distant Very lights traced patterns on the night sky. We had several hours of good, deep sleep. At first light the petrol cookers were lit and breakfast was soon ready.

Once more the plans were changed; we were now to act as escort to the divisional artillery. The column began a wide, semi-circular sweep southwards into the desert. On the way we passed several straggling columns of Italian prisoners, each escorted by only a handful of guards. In the afternoon we turned northwards towards the coast at Galal station.

Here some of our artillery units were firing in the direction we had just come from. This seemed ominous. We were told to dig in facing back to Daba, which we had by-passed in our sweep. We wondered what was going on. An agitated gunner officer rushed up. 'The whole German army is trapped down there,' he said rather melodramatically. We began to dig in the hope that even here we might be able to get a night's sleep. But the company commander shouted across, 'Get ready to move right away. We're going back to Daba to beat up a column of transport.' Some way back down the road we came upon several hundred stationary vehicles abandoned by their drivers. They were regularly spaced, many with their doors left open and some with their engines still running. We dismounted from our lorries and were ordered to comb the ground on each side of the road. 'B' Company was on the right and 'C' Company on the left. The colonel's car followed just behind us hugging the middle of the road, in wireless communication with Brigade.

By now darkness had fallen. Leading a section of carriers in front was Graham Jelley, the officer whose breakfast I had shared on the first morning. Every time he heard a sound he pumped a stream of bullets across the sand. He was too aggressive that night for my liking. 'C' Company took a few stray prisoners, but we encountered no one else. It soon became clear that we would not meet any further resistance, and the operation developed into a slow, blistering route march. We trudged for mile after mile. Our feet were feeling the strain and we were becoming extremely ill-tempered.

We had a short rest on the way, but when we started off again one man said that he could not go on as his feet were sore. I cursed him more harshly than I had anyone in the platoon before. The treatment was rough and ill-considered, but it worked. Then I went back to Halsall and told him that the whole thing was turning into a bloody farce. We had an angry set-to, whereupon Halsall stormed back to the colonel and presumably had a similar altercation with him. But we still plodded on.

At last we halted, and sat by the roadside to wait for the trucks to take us back. When we arrived at Galal it was too dark to find our own company positions; so we pulled off the road and decided to wait there until morning. We tried to dig in, but could make little impression on the solid ground. A Junkers 88 began to circle low overhead and sprayed us with taunting streams of tracer. Christ! Was there to be no respite even here? We piled loose stones around ourselves in an attempt to gain some protection before settling down to snatch some sleep in the few hours of the night that remained.

By morning things looked somewhat brighter. We drove

round to our old position, where breakfast was waiting. While we were eating, long columns of unescorted Italian prisoners appeared. These were the vehicle drivers we had been unable to find the night before; now they were coming in droves to give themselves up. They were rounded up at battalion headquarters and soon cleared away.

Perhaps, we thought, we should now have our long-awaited rest. But no. The company commander had some fresh orders. My platoon was to provide guards for the divisional prisoner of war cage. I flared up. 'For God's sake send someone else. Why must Ten Platoon always do everything?' We needed a break. How did we know what was in store for us tomorrow? And so I argued – unfairly and irrationally. But it was a normal reaction in the circumstances. I suppose that outbursts like this occurred in every company in every battle. Anyone working under strain will turn round at some time and curse the person above him, only to feel sheepish and repentant later.

We were taken to divisional headquarters, where three large, barbed-wire cages had been constructed: one for German other ranks, one for Italian officers and one for Italian other ranks. The military police were in charge, and the Germans were quickly loaded into lorries and driven back to base. Long columns of Italians were still arriving. Some were even driving their own vehicles and fussy senior officers were scratching around for their personal belongings. The men came pouring out of the vehicles, clutching suitcases, furniture, parcels of food and flasks of vino. A mass of scattered kit spilled out of the back of each vehicle. What the Italians themselves did not salvage our own men pilfered. It was an unedifying spectacle in the squalid chaos of defeat.

Inside the cages the prisoners were clamouring to be fed. The military police threw in water cans, which were snatched by a dozen eager arms. Cans of bully beef were seized in an undignified free-for-all the moment they were poked through the wire. Seeking to introduce some fairness into the distribution, the police tried tossing packets of large flat biscuits over the heads of the greedy ones in front to the poor wretches behind, who grovelled on their knees fighting for the prizes. The latrines were outside the wire and the prisoners were let out under escort in batches – with some frequency, for they were riddled with dysentery. When night came we posted guards. The babel inside the cages died down. The occupants curled up in their overcoats in the sand and slept. Soon it was silent everywhere. The sentries stayed alert but they need not have bothered: there was not an ounce of spirit left in those prisoners.

At dawn the Italian officers were removed in trucks, apart from two who were left behind. These were both medical officers and they were still wearing their Red Cross arm bands. I stopped them as they wandered disconsolately around the enormous compound. One was tall, haughty and uncommunicative. The other was a friendly little man, with dark sallow features, scruffy and unshaven, but with a typical conciliatory Italian smile and intelligent eyes. He spoke English and was eager to talk. He was carrying a paperback novel under his arm – an Italian translation of *The Stars Look Down*. 'Do you like Cronin?' I asked. 'Yes,' he replied solemnly. 'He is like Shakespeare, a pessimist – he paints life as it really is.' A strange hesitancy in his voice gave a studied, almost pompous, gravity to his words. His remarks intrigued me. Yet admittedly there was not much for him to feel optimistic about as he waited behind the barbed wire.

Trucks were arriving in large numbers. By mid-afternoon all the prisoners had been taken away and we were returned to the company. I was delighted to be told that there would be no move for at least twenty-four hours. At least we could take our boots off. It was sheer luxury to stretch out in stockinged feet once again. We slept like logs but at first light there was a harsh cry from company headquarters, 'Get dressed! Moving forward straight away.' We scrambled aboard the trucks in a flurry of blankets, equipment and boots, and drove away in desert formation towards the main road.

Troop carriers were supposed to travel on the open sand parallel with the road; but the attraction of a concrete surface was too great to be resisted and soon all the vehicles pulled on to the main coast road itself. The transport of the entire Eighth Army seemed to be packed nose to tail in a triumphant surging column – tank transporters, staff cars, ambulances and jeeps – all cutting in, overtaking and racing forward in an uncontrolled, disorderly mob. There were long halts and road blocks, but we managed to make some progress. One thing was certain: the Germans had suffered a crushing defeat. We passed hundreds of burnt-out tanks, wrecked and looted trucks, stiff corpses and an occasional smashed

94

aircraft. The railway which ran alongside the road was smashed to smithereens, the stations devastated and locomotives and carriages blown to pieces. Fuka airfield was flooded and scores of enemy planes grounded.

Whenever there was a halt the men jumped out and began to brew up; but invariably before they were ready there would be a curt command to move on. This happened about a dozen times with the men becoming progressively thirstier on each occasion. Finally, in desperation, they hurled the whole contraption, including the blazing petrol tin fire, into the back of the truck and brewed up as we went along. My reward for condoning these dangerous and illegitimate proceedings was a cup of delightful desert tea at the next halt.

By nightfall we had reached the plain outside Mersa Matruh. Next morning we were allotted a spacious company area near the town. By some caprice of the army supply system a quantity of pay arrived. I sat on the sand with a packing-case in front of me and the platoon ambled forward in a grinning, jocular line. It was the oddest of pay parades. The men stuffed the tattered Egyptian notes unconcernedly into their pockets. These were nothing but scraps of paper. For the first time in our lives we could see money in its true perspective. It was wonderful to be free for once from its tyranny.

There were no tasks given to us that day; we dug ourselves deep, comfortable slit trenches and rested. The night was also undisturbed. Next day, miraculously, there was still no move forward. Instead we were sent to help unload a shipment of petrol at the docks, which had been promptly opened in the wake of the advancing troops. We drove through the town to the water's edge, where the sunlight was playing around two forlorn-looking wrecks in the beautiful natural harbour of Matruh. The crates of petrol were hoisted from the hold and scudded down wooden rollers to the quay, to be packed into waiting lorries. It was a busy, strenuous morning, but well to our taste. At lunchtime we broke off to eat our haversack rations and took a furtive dip in the sea behind the breakwater.

Back at camp in the evening, we were told that there was still no move imminent. This time the information proved reliable. The company cooks had joined us and were sweating over their blazing petrol cookers. The rations were generous,

Captured German 88mm gun.

A crashed Stuka dive-bomber.

The aftermath of battle.

Column of prisoners surrendering through the smoke.

even including fresh meat, and were supplemented by welcome semi-official loot – highly ornamental brands of tinned vegetables and a surfeit of the exotic jams which the Germans seemed to have in such plenty. Overcoats and innumerable bundles of blankets had also arrived. This was comfort indeed.

We still conformed to the formalities of a military operation, standing-to in our slit trenches at dusk and dawn. At the first glimmer of light when the sentry wakened me I would go round and rouse the platoon. Though I shouted myself hoarse no one would budge. There was no alternative but to stir them into life by kicking each one in the ribs. Coughing and cursing, spitting and spluttering, the men would emerge from their grimy blankets and light their cigarette stubs. They would sit there shivering in the slit trenches, with one eye on the rising sun and the other on the cook's truck behind them. A new day had begun at Mersa Matruh.

The surrounding area had become much safer. Bombing had quite ceased. All day long, and for the best part of the night, streams of tanks, vehicles and heavy guns surged along the coast road to the front. One night we heard a mysterious whistle and an unmistakable puffing. The railway line had already been repaired and the first supply train was steaming up to Matruh.

A well was discovered nearby with any amount of water. We were advised not to drink it. Admittedly it tasted a little sweet – but that didn't worry us. On the third day we discovered that the Germans had thrown a dead Italian into the water to contaminate it. However, it still came in useful for washing clothes. An additional amenity was a mobile NAAFI canteen which arrived at brigade headquarters, enabling us to stock up with chocolate, tinned fruit and cigarettes.

We tackled a variety of odd jobs, salvaging enemy vehicles, stacking captured equipment and other such diversions. When work was over we were left to our own devices. This was the ideal life. Nobody worried us. There were no unnecessary parades, none of the irritating, outward formalities of discipline. Distinctions of rank scarcely existed. I lived and worked exclusively with the men and became completely identified with the platoon; we belonged to each

The author leading 'B' Company 4/5th Royal Sussex, in a march-past at Sidi Bishr, Alexandria, December 1942.

other. This was perhaps the happiest time of my whole army life.

At nightfall we would sit around and gossip. The men went over the battle again and again. Here the old soldiers' tales of the next generation were germinated. Reputations had been made and lost. Some were established as heroes; a few were tainted for ever.

News sheets were issued, along with maps showing the progress of the war; these had to be explained to the men. The unexpected news of the landings at the other end of North Africa was enthusiastically received. We were told that it was not possible for all Eighth Army units to take part in the pursuit battle, for supply problems restricted the size of the forces that could be maintained. Some units would therefore have to stay behind for the time being. Our division was one of these. This information was followed by the army commander's 'message to the troops', which reminded us of the earlier injunction about 'hitting the enemy for six out of Africa' and summed up what had been achieved in the battle. The message concluded: 'Our task is not finished yet; the Germans are out of Egypt but there are still some left in

North Africa. There is some good hunting to be had further to the West . . . On with the task and good hunting to you all. As in all pursuits some have to remain behind to start with; but we shall all be in it before the finish.'

Communications of this kind always sounded totally artificial and irrelevant to front-line troops. How could any activity as revolting as war possibly be presented to the actual participants in sporting terms? What is more, here we were in the platoon thoroughly enjoying our brief rest, congratulating ourselves heartily on this unexpected change in our fortunes, and we were supposed to be upset at being left behind. What a load of humbug!

One day when the platoon was out working the sky suddenly darkened and a heavy shower of rain fell, drenching our clothes and blankets and flooding the slit trenches. That night a rum issue was authorised and I was sent to the officers' mess at battalion headquarters to collect the company's ration. I found the mess tent in the darkness and pushed my way confidently inside. The assembled company were on the point of sitting down to dinner, and there could not have been a worse moment to arrive. I wished them all good evening. After a long pause, someone spoke. What did I want? I had come to fetch the rum ration for 'B' Company, I explained. The quartermaster slowly detached himself from the others and, taking me on one side, lifted a flap near the entrance and handed me a large brown stone jar without a word. The atmosphere was chilly; somehow there was generated in that draughty tent all the frigid formality of a ceremonial mess dinner. I was an unwelcome intruder and, seizing the jar, I escaped with relief into the darkness, back to the company lines, to Halsall, and to the warm, ungrudging friendliness of the men.

Next day we were given bivouacs, which we used to provide rough shelters over our slit trenches. It was just as well, for a storm arose at midday and clouds of sand whipped around us all afternoon. The sand seeped through every crevice in the canvas, though it was tolerable enough under cover, sitting with a blanket wrapped round one. Cross had salvaged a book for me, a tattered copy of *Jane Eyre*, and I soon lost myself in the enchantment of the story. Action left one with a sense of anti-climax. The body welcomed the rest and the senses were gratified, but the mind was fallow and craved a stimulant. How I seized upon this novel. It is a mistake to imagine that war erodes one's sensibilities. Now that the numbing effect of battle had faded, I was more than ever responsive to each shade of meaning in the book and the tears trickled down my gritty cheeks on to the pages.

A few days later, towards the end of November, the officers were called together and told about our future. The division was being disbanded and the brigade split up. The 2nd Battalion were to become paratroops; we on the other hand were to move early in the New Year to join the Persia and Iraq Force. We would be known henceforward as the 4/5th Royal Sussex, since the ill-fated 4th Battalion, which had been virtually wiped out in the battle, was not being reconstituted. In Persia the army was facing a threat from the north, where German troops in southern Russia had penetrated as far as the Caucasus. Our role would be to protect the oil wells and the supply route to Russia.

Persia and Iraq, 1943–4
Scale one inch = 175 miles

Part Three: Persia and Iraq

9

In anticipation of the move to Persia we were shifted back to Alexandria, where we tasted civilised pleasures once again and revelled in the unabashed pursuit of physical comfort. On the first free evening there was the luxury of a perfumed shampoo, the ecstasy of a hot, steaming bath at the Windsor Palace and the joy of dinner at the Union Bar – onion soup, *fillet de sole bonne femme* and roast quail. Alexandria by night was pure magic after the barren solitudes of the desert. It was a city of teeming mystery and strange street cries, its pavements thronged with jostling natives, whose dark faces were transfigured by the fiery, flashing brilliance of the electric trams.

Our camp was on the outskirts at Sidi Bishr, near the sea, in a conventional Egyptian setting of sand dunes and palm trees. There was a NAAFI and a cinema close by and frequent trains into the centre of the city. Officers slept in tents, real 180-pounders you could actually stand up in. A central officers' mess was established, in an elegant marquee, for all the officers in the battalion. A three-ton lorry was driven discreetly to the base depot, returning with our tin trunks; and service dress reappeared in the evenings. In camp the regimental sergeant-major reasserted his dominion over the men. Church parades were instituted, as well as a ceremonial guard mounting. Saluting and formalities of discipline were rigorously revived.

As the regular pattern of regimental life was resumed the battalion began to manifest a distinctive identity. Formerly, it had been a territorial unit, centred in Hastings and recruited locally. Despite some dilution since 1939 it had retained in speech and style a strong flavour of the South Downs. Among the officers was a fair sprinkling of professional men, solicitors and preparatory schoolmasters mainly, and the inflections and cynicism of Oxford mingled with the homelier rural accents and more sanguine disposition of the other ranks.

In the closing months of the year there was an epidemic of jaundice among the troops in the Middle East. I was smitten in mid-December and spent Christmas Day 1942 in the Military General Hospital in Alexandria, and New Year's Day conveniently in the nearby Scottish Home for Convalescent Officers. When I rejoined the battalion they were at Quassassin, a staging area in the Delta, making final preparations for the move. News greeted me on my arrival that I was being transferred from 'B' Company to Headquarter Company to become mortar officer. The prospect of a new and interesting job was an attraction, but it was painful to leave the platoon. The bond forged in the last few months was strong and curiously tender. I felt distinctly mean and mercenary when it came to saying goodbye. To the men Ten Platoon was everything. Their roots were here and this was their home; most of them would never serve anywhere else. They could not comprehend how anyone who had once settled in the platoon should ever consent to leave it. But I still went.

Just before the departure from Quassassin I was diverted on a three weeks' mortar course to the Middle East Infantry Training Centre at Deir Suneid in Palestine. With John Martin, a lieutenant from 'A' Company who was going on a weapon training course, and a new batman called Hinkins, I picked up the night train from Cairo. We crossed the Sinai in darkness, breakfasted at Quantara at four in the morning, and alighted on the platform at Deir Suneid halt as dawn was breaking and a light drizzle falling. We drove in trucks to the hutted camp, which was just off the main road running north from Gaza.

Palestine proved delightful after the barren monotony of Egypt. Everything was so much sweeter and fresher. Rolling mounds of sand were interwoven with patches of crops and green pasture-land, and clumps of trees and flowers. The abundant orange groves were laden with a surfeit of golden fruit; and there were farmsteads with cheerful peasants and even strolling cows in leafy lanes.

At the school we trained vigorously on the 3-inch mortar, flinging the barrel around and stamping on the base-plate in the approved fashion. Our spare moments were spent memorising training pamphlets. In the evenings after dinner we usually visited the camp cinema, a draughty contraption of wood and corrugated iron. Huddled on collapsible wooden benches, overcoat collars turned up, with a bar of Palestinian chocolate apiece and the weekly free supply of pipe tobacco, we savoured the latest of Hollywood's cultural offerings.

Weekends were free, and one Saturday afternoon John Martin and I made for Jerusalem. First we travelled south to Gaza, a good centre for hitch-hiking. There in the market place we got a lift in the back of a large open Australian lorry. Perched high on a pile of canvas assault boats and cricket pads we had a breezy drive northwards along the plain towards the distant circle of mountains. As darkness fell the lorry laboured up a winding road through rocky hills that seemed framed for ambush, and then descended steeply down into the valley to Jerusalem. After dinner in the King David Hotel, which overlooked the Old City, we found a bed for the night in a nearby boarding house.

On Sunday morning we travelled to Bethlehem in a crowded Arab bus. There the Church of the Nativity, despite the ravages of two thousand years, proved to be a building of solid and sombre permanence, and still very much a living shrine. The guardianship of the church was scrupulously divided between the main Christian sects, and in the eyes of these priests there glowed an almost mediaeval fanaticism. In every corner of the gloomy vaults one could recapture, in a way no longer possible in the West, a sense of the mysticism, intolerance and power of a religion embedded in the blood, as much as in the spirit, of its devotees.

In the afternoon, following a walk on the Mount of Olives and in the Garden of Gethsemane, we explored the Old City of Jerusalem, compact within its high stone walls and little changed since the time of Christ. There were the same bare stone buildings and narrow cobbled streets with open-fronted shop stalls, mingling crowds of Jews and Arabs, wandering donkeys and heaps of garbage. We visited the Wailing Wall and paid our respects to the Church of the Holy Sepulchre. Finally, outside the city gates, we found an enterprising Arab taxi driver who was persuaded, after a somewhat undignified haggle, to drive us in comfort all the way back to the camp.

When the course was over we set out by train for Persia to join the battalion. The main line ran as far as Haifa, where we changed to an antiquated train that meandered across Palestine into Trans-Jordan and then up a twisting track through the Syrian mountains to Damascus. At three in the morning the station was wet, black and deserted. We were taken by truck to the transit camp, a muddy and cheerless hovel. By dawn, however, the rain had stopped and the city looked beautiful in the early sunlight, with dazzling white terraced buildings inlaid on the reddish-brown mountain face. The next stage of the journey was a twenty-hour drive across the desert by Nairn bus, a powerful luxury coach. We set off in the early afternoon and soon left the main concrete road, striking due east across the hard desert track for the rest of the day and through the night. At midnight we trooped out of the coach at dismal Fort Rutba for a cup of tea in the dirtiest of wayside cafés. Then we were on our way again until dawn, for breakfast at Ramadi. By mid-morning, with some relief, we reached the outskirts of Baghdad.

From there our route lay north to Khanaqin, near the border between Iraq and Persia. We travelled by night in an Indian-type sleeper train, arriving at four in the morning. The station was at a railhead, so we were able to sleep in the compartment until daybreak, when the obliging Iraqi guard brought tea and hot water from the engine for shaving. After sending a message to the battalion to let them know where we were, we took a stroll through the streets.

Khanaqin was an undistinguished township with narrow smelly streets, mud houses and grubby shops piled high with exotic fruit and vegetables, as well as myriads of silver trinkets. It was enclosed on three sides by plantations of stunted palms – the only vegetation; on the fourth lay a low sandy mound, serving as a cemetery, with rows and rows of diminutive earthen graves. The rest of the surrounding land was flat and barren, but mountains rose in the distance to the north and east. By the time we returned to the station a truck was waiting for us. Our road ran eastwards into the foothills, following the traditional caravan route from Baghdad to Teheran. The battalion camp was about twelve miles away at Qasr-i-Shirin, just across the frontier into Persia.

The battalion was now in the 6th Indian Division and formed part of the 27th Indian Infantry Brigade, along with troops from the Guides and Baluch Regiments. The whole division was encamped in a gigantic plain on the fringes of the foothills. From a distance the white dotted formations of symmetrically spaced tents were a stirring sight, looking much as Alexander's army must have looked in antiquity on this same Persian soil. Rearing up in the background were the jagged peaks of the Bandi-Baz-Diraz range; beyond, crouching in sullen majesty, were the immense snow-capped mountains of the interior.

When we arrived the camp was deserted; the battalion was away on an exercise. We dropped our baggage in the sleeping tents and made for the officers' mess to pick up our accumulated mail. The mess was in a large dug-out, with shallow earthen walls and a sloping tent roof. Through a tumble-down doorway a few rickety steps led down inside, where there were some bare wooden trestle tables, a few canvas chairs, an improvised bar and a litter of out-of-date copies of *Punch* and the *Illustrated London News*. Though hardly the last word in civilised comfort, at least it was a home.

In recent weeks several more officers had joined the unit, and Vincent Dishman, Hugh Horsley and Charles Freeman proved to be kindred spirits. In the ensuing months, while we newcomers hardly felt ourselves to be part of the inner circle, we found a congenial niche among the more boisterous subalterns in the mess. We always sat at the bottom of the dinner table where the ribaldry was uninhibited, out of earshot of the colonel and his more courtly intimates at the top. After dinner, when the élite had drifted off to play bridge by the light of smoky paraffin lamps, the rest of us squatted around the valor oil stoves gossiping, cracking walnuts and draining our meagre ration of NAAFI spirits.

Thus we spent the winter evenings, cheerfully enough, in this remote and desolate environment. Outside, when the mess closed and the last lamps in the tents were extinguished, the darkness was absolute and the silence broken only by the distant howling of jackals and the occasional mad rush of a pack of wild, snarling pai-dogs through the camp.

The main nocturnal hazard was the windstorms, which usually blew up in the early hours. A hurricane could spring from nowhere and dominate the plain in next-to-no time. Every tent would then be menaced by the perverse and undiscriminating blast. There was no pleasure to compare with that of lying in bed listening to the click of the mallet and the agitated hum of voices that told of some senior officer whose tent had come to grief in the neighbourhood. But the delights of self-congratulation could be short-lived. After an ominous creaking of the tent pegs, an unnatural tension of the guys and a splintering of the pole, the whole panoply of canvas, wood and rope could suddenly collapse, leaving one to struggle out, cursing and shivering, through the wreckage.

There were some terrible thunderstorms, too, when the plain was lit with flash after flash of lightning and the sombre mountains reverberated with peals of deafening thunder. Torrential rain would cascade down incessantly, flooding the wadis and sending streams of sandy water coursing through the camp. We could not escape the fury of these storms, living as we did with only the thickness of a canvas sheet between us and the elements. The tents were dug in for warmth but they leaked badly, and even if one succeeded in sleeping through the storm the floor would be inches deep by morning. The officers at least had camp beds, but for the men conditions were pitiable. They slept on the floor, and their blankets and clothes got drenched. They only had one suit of battledress apiece and one pair of boots, and when these were wet there was nothing they could do but sit around in gym shorts and canvas shoes, praying for sunshine. When the sun finally came out in mocking splendour, the men just spread out their soaking clothes in the open to dry. After a storm the battalion would spend the whole of the next day drying clothes, draining off the water and clearing away the debris.

The mess was always a casualty after heavy rainstorms and one day it was flooded beyond redemption. The tent had to be dismantled and re-erected on level ground beside the original site. The old dug-out, a foot deep in water with only the piles of stones that had supported the flagpoles showing above the surface, was derelict, looking for all the world like some overgrown, classical ruin.

Our working days at Qasr-i-Shirin were spent in training, with regular battalion and brigade exercises. These took place over much the same terrain and we soon became familiar with every yard of ground in the vicinity of the camp. The various features came to be inseparably associated with the exploits of particular officers, such as the sandy hillock called 'Kitson's Folly' and a wadi known as 'Evans's Jump'. The exercises were highly repetitious, following as they did the routine cycle of advance to contact, attack and defence. Neil Cairncross, the intelligence officer, summed up the inevitability of these manoeuvres at the start of an exercise late one afternoon. He was 'putting us in the picture' while we waited expectantly for the CO to return with orders from the brigadier. After pointing out the main features on the ground he said, 'The enemy is on Kitson's Folly, approximately two companies strong. The brigade is deployed along Evans's Jump, the Guides on the left and the Baluch on the right. The battalion is in reserve and it is just possible,' he added gravely, 'that we may be called upon to do a night attack.'

This particular exercise, like the others, petered out to its inevitable conclusion at dawn, when the welcome signal to close came from Brigade. The officers' mess truck duly arrived over the skyline. Before returning to camp we sat in dignity at a trestle table in the early morning sunshine eating our breakfast of soya links, while walnut sellers from the nearby village in their tattered sheepskin coats, tight-fitting skull caps and bare brown feet, hovered around begging for scraps.

When spring approached and the days lengthened, it became much warmer and mosquitoes began to whine at night. Early in April preparations were made for moving camp to Kermanshah in the mountains. We travelled eastwards in a long convoy. A bitumen surface was being laid along the road but so far it extended only a few miles beyond Qasr-i-Shirin. We soon overtook the melancholy engineering party, with their tar barrels and sprayers. Beyond this, the surface of the road was soft and uneven, and pitted by the heavy traffic. Besides the dusty convoys of military vehicles, there were civilian lorries – big black six-wheelers from the UKCC, the United Kingdom Commercial Corporation, which was responsible for supplies to Russia. The drivers were Persians, culled from among the more civilised townsmen, but they were mechanically immature and drove their machines recklessly, tearing the road to pieces as they went. Here and there by the roadside as we passed were gangs of road-repairers, ragged and outlandish-looking fellows with seven-foot shovels, impatiently waiting to toss another heap of gravel into the ruts as soon as we had gone.

On the road we also passed several straggling columns of

Vehicle convoy winding through the Paitak Pass into Persia.

nomads. Like us they were on the move from the plains to the uplands to avoid the intolerable summer heat. Driven by instinct, like migratory birds, they felt this deep intuitive call each spring. These motley bands of surly natives had inexpressive faces, like leather. Their grim, flat-chested womenfolk rode side-saddle on overladen donkeys, with the poultry perched behind on the donkeys' rumps and the rest of the livestock trailing in the rear. The men tramped alongside, dark and sullen, thrashing the donkeys pitilessly with large sharp sticks. Yet, there was a fierce and haughty virility about these men who, tempered by extremes of climate, were lean and hard as steel.

As the convoy approached the main face of the mountain range the vehicles toiled slowly upwards in a serpentine column along the looping road towards the summit and through the narrow Paitak pass – the gateway into the heart of Persia. The top was crested with 'dragons' teeth' and improvised tank traps, relics of the invasion of Persia the year before. Beyond lay a wide, open plain, radiant in the sunlight and surrounded by sheltering mountains. We leaguered for the night at the edge of the road, sleeping beside our vehicles.

A desolating wind swept across the plain and we were glad of our extra blankets. At dawn we moved off again. After passing through the town of Shahbad we were faced with another long climb. The hugeness of the landscape took one's breath away – vast raking mountains enfolding tremendous stretches of plain, which were chequered with patches of ploughland, crops and grass.

On the outskirts of Kermanshah the road swung north-wards, by-passing the town until it came to a vast face of brown rock, half-covered in snow. Then it turned abruptly eastwards, as though flinching from this solid, looming mass. We followed the road for five or six miles along the foot of the range towards the point where the crest culminated in the huge Bisitun mountain, bearing the ageless rock-carvings of Darius. The site of the camp was on a narrow grass strip between the road and the mountains. Some of the tents had already been erected in neat lines by the advance party and we promptly set about pitching the rest of them. For a couple of days everyone was busy with mallet and shovel.

The mountains behind were inviting and Hugh Horsley and I took an early opportunity of going for a climb. The range was so extensive that the heights were deceptive. The plain itself was five thousand feet above sea level, and the mountains reached ten thousand, so this sweep of rock rising from our own back garden was higher than the highest mountain in Britain. We were left in no doubt about this when a brisk afternoon's tramp up the winding tracks took us barely half-way to the snow-line.

At Kermanshah there was the same regular cycle of training exercises, but the terrain was more varied and challenging. The mortars were in great demand, especially in field firing exercises when we acted as artillery. And a splendidly hearty and inaccurate artillery we were, calculated to enliven even the most prosaic of company exercises. The platoon was equipped with Bren gun carriers, and these always provided an exhilarating drive as the tracks thundered across open country and one stood beside the driver with the wind streaming past one's face. By now the countryside was at its most picturesque. The snows were beginning to disappear from the mountain tops. The fields were full of waving golden crops, speckled with rebellious vermilion poppies, and bee-eaters with their kaleidoscopic tints were flitting through the brilliant sunshine. The landscape was cloaked in all the bright, exotic colours of the early Persian summer.

Life in camp was a strangely insulated existence for the eight hundred of us. No one else came near, and we hardly ever set eyes on a stranger, except for a few natives. Yet within this closely-knit community the standard of discipline was high, with meticulous saluting and minute inspections of the guards and sentries who patrolled the perimeter by day and night. Social life revolved around three centres – the men's canteen, the sergeants' mess and the officers' mess. In our own mess, in a far corner of the camp, the requirements of protocol were carefully observed even in these primitive surroundings. There was a formal dinner each evening, at which we all maintained a cautious reserve towards the colonel. But when the meal was over and the CO had retired for the night, quite often an impromptu party would develop, sometimes lasting until the small hours when we would stumble away inebriated to our tents.

To each subaltern in turn fell the chore of duty officer. This involved remaining tolerably sober at dinner, with a view to turning out the guard later and inspecting the sentries at some uncertain hour of the night. It also entailed sleeping beside the field telephone in the adjutant's office. The nights were stifling now and the tent was always swarming with insect life – crickets, moths, mantises and mosquitoes – but it was roomy enough and a sanctuary of privacy in the crowded and noisy camp. At ten o'clock precisely, by which time the canteen was closed and the general hubbub stilled, there would be a crunch of footsteps on the path outside the tent, a pause, and then the bugle would ring out with the crisp clear notes of the Last Post, expressing in its forlorn beauty all the melancholy of life in these lonely and forsaken stations overseas.

One day a few of us were lucky enough to be chosen for a short leave trip to Teheran. We travelled in the back of a fifteen hundred-weight truck on the two-day journey through Sultanabad and Qum – a city of mosques with golden domes and blue minarets – across vast white salt flats and along the straight and dusty highway to the capital. Towering behind the city was Demavend, surely the most beautiful single mountain in the world, its exquisite classical contours and snow-capped peak standing in unchallenged isolation on the skyline.

Teheran, the Paris of the Middle East, was a city of wide boulevards and sparkling streams that gushed down the roadsides, and gardens full of trees and flowers; a city of contrasts, though, for tucked away behind were areas of reeking slums. Persia was in many ways the most backward and poverty-stricken of all the Middle East countries, yet it seemed to retain the greatest sense of dignity and independence even under occupation. In Teheran, for all the dominating foreign influences, military and commercial, Persia proper contrived to keep herself to herself.

Our few days in the city were spent roaming the bazaars and lounging in the palatial club which the English colony made open to us. When the time came to leave we stocked up with vodka, caviare, cheeses and even carpets for the mess. We took the more northerly route home through Kasvin and Hamadan, formerly Ecbatana the ancient capital of the Medes, where we stayed the night in an antique balconied hotel in the heart of the congested town. Next day we arrived back at the battalion to be greeted with news of an impending move.

10

After Kermanshah came Kifri, in the sweltering plains of Iraq. We travelled in June, suitably attired in light-weight clothing and observing the standing Paiforce summer regulation of 'Topees west of Paitak'. The convoy followed the main road back through Qasr-i-Shirin and Khanaqin, turning westwards near Jaloula into the plain. We drove across the flat, hard, reddish desert for two hours to Kifri camp, a patch of sand in the middle of nowhere. We had had some forewarning of conditions there from the advance party of the battalion changing places with us, but we were not prepared for the intense heat which struck us on arrival. It was midday and the exposed plain was raked by a remorseless sun.

At Kifri it was impossible to work in the heat of the day through the midsummer months that followed. Reveille each morning was at five, and we trained for an hour before breakfast, resuming afterwards until ten. Thereafter only light duties under cover were possible, for by then the vehicles and weapons standing in the open could no longer be touched – the metal was scorching hot. Most of the officers stayed in the company office tents until noon, reading pamphlets and flicking idly through the latest Army Council Instructions and Paiforce General Orders. Then it was time for 'tiffin' in the mess. The officers' mess was a fragile, shell construction with a canvas roof and flimsy chattai matting

walls; at the entrance stood two enormous earthenware jars filled with cold water. The meal usually consisted of thinly cut spam and a large slice of melon.

We made no pretence of working in the afternoons, but skulked in our sleeping tents, which were dug in around the mess. We lay naked on our camp beds, stewing in the awful pits which were our homes. By August the recorded temperatures in Baghdad were stabbing towards 120 degrees Fahrenheit and in the Kifri plains they were certainly higher. There was a wind that rose daily in the afternoons but offered

Jerusalem, 1942.

no relief, for this was the 'date-ripener', a hot breeze from the south, like the fumes from an oven. It carried with it sand, grit and filth, which seeped through the tent flaps, coating our sweating bodies with a layer of grime and soiling our saturated clothes. There was no refuge either from the thick black plague of buzzing flies that stuck to our limbs and faces. It was impossible to sleep or read; one could only stretch out and pray for nightfall. Small wonder that as the weeks passed people began to disappear into hospital with dysentery and heat stroke.

The evenings, if only by way of contrast, were pleasant. We were able to do a little work between five and seven and sometimes for a few hours later, in the cooler conditions after dark. The more ambitious subalterns, absenting themselves from dinner in the call of duty, usually contrived to hold their platoon exercises in the vicinity of the mess to impress the CO. It was the practice at night for the meal to be served in the open outside the mess tent on trestle tables lit by oil pressure lamps. At intervals parties of stretcher-bearers would trudge past through the gathering gloom, and anti-tank guns would be manhandled unnervingly close to the diners. On the rare occasions when the mortars were needed for night-firing on the nearby range, I always took care to time the first rounds for 7.30pm precisely, when the padre would just about be saying grace.

Our one recreation at Kifri, strangely enough, was cricket. An ingenious sergeant made a wicket out of hessian tent bags, which were spread on the sand, watered and rolled flat with an oil drum full of pebbles. From a group of enthusiasts we organised an officers-versus-sergeants match, and later with a combined team ventured as far as Baghdad to play Baghdad Casuals. This was a local side made up of expatriate civilians from the oil companies and banks, and a few staff officers from GHQ. The match was played over two evenings and in the afternoons we enjoyed the amenities of the opulent Alwiyah Club, with its luxurious green-tiled swimming pool. The game ended in a draw with honours even, but for me the trip was marred by an attack of dysentery. This persisted even after returning to camp and a few days later I was admitted to hospital.

Kifri Military Hospital was another tented establishment in the open plain, but equipped with electric fans, shower baths improvised from punctured petrol cans, and a refrigerator for cool drinks in every ward. After three restful weeks I was pronounced well and sent for a fortnight's convalescence to a leave camp at Karind in the mountains, where the climate was bracing, the curries superb and there was time at last to read *War and Peace* from cover to cover in comfort. Then, fully cured and rested, I returned to the battalion.

Impatient by now to get back, I approached the camp in high spirits. The mess looked so familiar and inviting. But, once inside, I was disconcerted to find five new officers making themselves at home and hailing the corporal behind the bar with nonchalant familiarity. Imperceptibly over the months the mess with its web of friendships had become something precious; an intrusion on this scale was a threat to its character and stability. I recognised now the fundamental justice of the invisible barrier which always faced new entrants. No doubt the newcomers would all be assimilated in time, but in the coming weeks, notwithstanding the general affability and bonhomie, each of them would be on probation, under a close and subtle scrutiny.

Within a week the battalion was on the move again, by train to Musaiyib, a big supply centre forty miles south of Baghdad between the Tigris and the Euphrates and a few miles from the ruins of Babylon. Our task was the depressing one of guarding installations, a base workshop, an ordnance depot and an ammunition dump. The climate was sluggish and enervating and the place infested with sandfly, from which we all contracted fever in turn. As numbers were reduced through sickness, the burden of guard duties fell more heavily on those who were left, until almost the entire battalion was needed on guard each night. The tenacity and cunning of the native thieves was remarkable, to say nothing of their physical courage; for it was the policy to shoot to kill, and we had live booby traps around the perimeter wires. Nonetheless, they contrived to break in somewhere every night and we never seemed to catch anyone.

It was a dismal station and a life of boring routine; for the men guard after guard, and for the officers a ceaseless round of inspections by day and night. There was the prospect of three or four months of this appalling monotony, when the glad news reached me that I was to be appointed battalion

Battalion camp at Qasr-i-shirin, Persia.

intelligence officer and in preparation for this sent on a course to Cairo.

Neil Cairncross, who was also going to Cairo on a course, travelled with me and we spent a day or two with one of our companies on detachment in Baghdad. The city was hateful in summer, with its crowded, smelly streets. Fat Iraqis sprawled outside their dirty shops, and the place had an atmosphere of lassitude and hopelessness. It was a great relief to escape on the Pullman bus across the desert towards Damascus. A day later we were in a new world, one that was fresh and full of promise. Plantations of orange trees led to the clean, bright town, with its washed cobbles and sparkling buildings. The streets resounded with the bustling clatter from the clogs of citizens in baggy blue breeches.

From Damascus, we took a ramshackle train, which circled down the twisting mountain passes into Palestine. At each halt the carriages were invaded by swarms of children, carrying baskets of Jaffa oranges and enormous grapefruit. We had an overnight stop at Haifa. Next day the train ran alongside the golden, sandy shores of the blue Mediterranean. After an uncomfortable ride through the night across the Sinai desert we approached Cairo towards noon.

Cairo was the oriental city par excellence. The very name conjured up a vision of dark streets with deep secrets, and all the violent extremes of Eastern life: fanatical excesses of religious asceticism on the one hand, and on the other depths of depravity and perversions unimagined in the West. Now that the tide of war had receded along the coast of North Africa, and through Sicily into Italy, Cairo no longer had the vital military importance of a year or so before. Yet the city still dominated the Middle East, with an air of permanence and immutability far transcending its cursory involvement in our own vulgar and ephemeral brawl.

At the railway station the porters, wearing coarse blue smocks like orphan children at home, descended on us with brutal efficiency. They hustled us away in a flurry of suitcases and a tumult of protestations. Outside, the hawkers with their baskets were chanting the familiar cry, 'Eggsa bread – eggsa bread', and the streets rang with the paper sellers' shouts of 'Egypta Mail – Egypta Mail' and the croaking, guttural 'Bourse'. We pressed through the milling crowd to a waiting taxi, drawn, as if by a magnet, to Shepheard's Hotel.

Shepheard's was quite unlike any other hotel. It had the cloistered dignity of a cathedral, with its enormous domed ceiling, rich stained glass windows, sumptuously tapestried armchairs and glittering displays of glassware. There was no trace of anything cheap or gaudy or flashy; just an impression of solid, unornamented wealth. Nothing could compare with the somnolent peace of the lounge that afternoon as we sank into the depths of those enormous easy chairs. In the evening the hotel sprang into throbbing activity. Though it was filled at the time with numbers of Europeans, it remained essentially Eastern and was the focal point of Cairo society. Distinguished-looking Arabs in flowing dress came and went freely and were very much at home, and the lounges were full of tall, elegant Egyptian women. It was on this spot that Napoleon had had his headquarters; Rommel had planned to settle here when he took the Delta. Though the ramifications of modern war had obliged our own GHQ to seek accommodation in a larger building, senior officers still gravitated here in their off-duty hours. Shepheard's continued to be the spiritual home of the Middle East Force.

The Intelligence Centre was at Helwan, some ten miles south of Cairo beside the River Nile. The school was in a hutted camp, with a comfortable mess and a room each for the students. The syllabus consisted of talks and demonstrations in the lecture hall, a variety of intelligence problems to be worked out individually or in syndicates, and occasional simulated exercises in the open with wireless and field telephones in the scrubby sand along the river bank. We spent most evenings in our rooms, memorising details of the organisation, equipment and insignia of the German army. But each Saturday was free and then we made a bee-line for Cairo.

There, after a leisurely round of drinks at Shepheard's or the more garish Continental Hotel, and a meal at the *Auberge de Turf* or the *Petit Coin de France*, we normally finished up for the night at Doll's Cabaret. At Doll's you sat at the bar or danced with the artistes who hovered around. After a dance it was customary to repay your partner with a drink, the 'artiste's special', which was twice the normal price and little more than coloured water. When the bar closed at ten o'clock you could only buy 'champagne' at three pounds a bottle, or cider at ten shillings a glass.

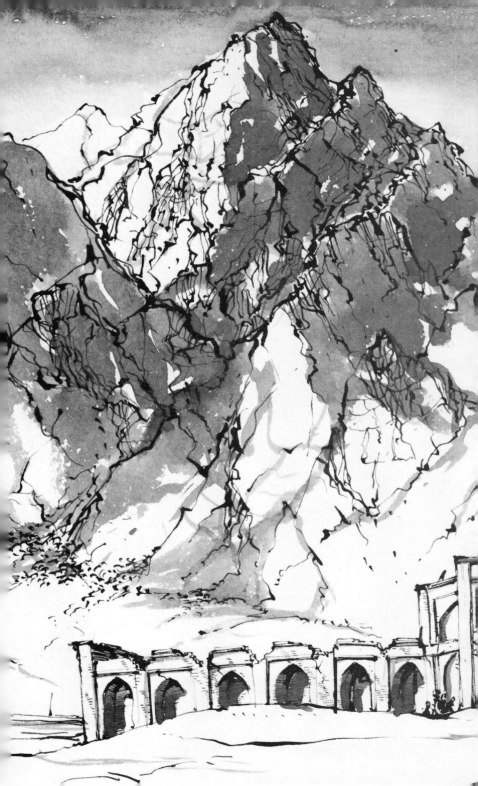

Bisitun, near Kermanshah, Persia.

One Saturday night I made a set for Ilona, a melancholy Hungarian divorcée – or maybe she had done away with her husband, I forget which. She had deep, enormous eyes, and was intelligent and sympathetic. She had another military suitor, an American airman, and we took it in turns to dance with her on the crowded floor. When Ilona had to slip away to take part in the cabaret, the American and I joined forces at the bar. 'You don't look like a sucker,' he said to me, grinning, by way of flattering introduction.

For some reason the talk turned to politics. He was bitterly opposed to Roosevelt, which rather shocked me. 'As far as I am concerned, George Washington's the best President we ever had,' he said, and thus we chatted while Ilona performed. We were joined by another friend of his, an objectionable little Yankee officer. He was very drunk and muttered, 'I got the Distinguished Flying Cross . . . I got seven victories in combat . . . and I got photographs to prove it.' Then he glanced at me and carried on, 'I've flown your fuck'n Hurricanes. I've flown your fuck'n Spitfires. And I've never seen a fucking Englishman who could do anything I couldn't do.' He was revolting. But his friend smiled tolerantly and brushed his remarks aside. 'Oh, Joe!' he explained, 'Of course, he just hates Englishmen.' This one was so different from his bumptious friend; but even he went on to say pointedly, 'I hate the English too.' Then he added quickly, 'Of course, you're not English, you come from Wales.' 'But,' I protested, 'I'm English.' 'No. No,' he said. 'Welsh, Scots or Irish – they're different, they're OK . . . but the English! Now take Churchill – he's a typical Englishman.'

Somehow one always began well with these people, but then their picking, insidious criticism would provoke one into a blustering jingoism. To avoid the temptation I sought refuge in the lavatory. But there was no escape. An American sergeant buttonholed me. He was being thrown out of the building, as Doll's was for commissioned ranks only. He protested, 'Hey Cap'n! You're allowed in here because you're an officer. I'm an enlisted man – so I can't come in. But I'm as good a man as you are any day.' All this brassy equalitarianism was too much! When I thought of the easy relationship between the platoon and myself at Mersa Matruh, and compared it with this shoddy slogan democracy

I was furious. I told the sergeant, 'Listen, brother, I was an enlisted man long before you ever went near the army.' Pointing to my pips I added, 'These don't grow on gooseberry bushes, you know. It took me eighteen months' bloody hard work to get a commission – I recommend you to do the same.'

Back at the bar I was relieved to find that Ilona had returned. She was a nice girl, albeit professional. It was good to be close to a woman again after so long and to murmer sweet nothings in broken French in the middle of that thrusting, jazzy mob. What went on, I wondered, in the mind of that soulful and enigmatic goddess as she contemplated night after night the procession of garrulous and drunken boys who passed through Doll's, pouring their money away like water. It was clear that she had her private intrigues. A morose barman leaned over as he was serving a drink and muttered in an intense whisper, '*Mademoiselle, vous savez que mes sentiments pour vous sont toujours les mêmes.*' She shook her head indifferently and he vanished to the other end of the bar. She turned back to me. But at the end of the evening when I asked if I could take her home, she gave a knowing smile, apologised most sweetly and hurried away to her Egyptian boyfriend, who was waiting in a car outside.

The three weeks of the course passed all too quickly and soon I was on the return journey to Iraq, back to the unwelcome prospect of Musaiyib once more. On arrival, however, I found preparations being made for a move.

The battalion was to relieve the Guides Regiment guarding the oil wells at Kirkuk in Northern Iraq. At least this promised to be more interesting than those dreadful lifeless dumps at Musaiyib. The move was accelerated when orders arrived from GHQ to complete it within twenty-four hours. Mullah Mustapha, leader of a band of Kurdish outlaws, had started a rebellion in the mountains. A punitive expedition – a brigade of the Iraqi army – had failed to suppress the revolt. Meanwhile in the closing months of 1943 the Mullah, unopposed, was striking at the isolated police posts one by one. He was threatening Diyana, a village just north of the Rowanduz gorge with Christian inhabitants – the wives of soldiers in the Iraq Levies. We had to send a section of carriers and later a mobile column commanded by Graham Jelley to protect them. The rest of the battalion, after the overnight move, settled down to more mundane duties, mounting guards over the various oil installations in the Kirkuk oil field. In the north the revolt soon began to fizzle out; the Mullah showed little inclination to become involved with British troops. There was even an exchange of courtesies at Christmas between the rebels and our detachment. The scare soon died down.

Early in the New Year I was sent to Cairo on another course – at Heliopolis this time – on the interpretation of air photographs. Coming so quickly after the previous visit, the second trip was something of an anti-climax. The course itself was amusing enough since it involved playing with steroscopes and photographs of military equipment and installations, and dabbling in trigonometry. But living in the closed community of a battalion tended to make one somewhat intolerant and conservative. The novelty of being with strangers soon palled and adjusting to yet another fresh set of companions was an effort. There were no regrets this time when the course came to an end and I returned to Iraq.

By now the battalion had moved again, to Khanaqin, where there were more oil wells to be guarded. The mess tent was in a dugout with a shingle floor, a huge tar-barrel stove burning crude oil in the centre of the room and oil pressure lamps for lighting. On the evening I got back there was an unexpected delivery of strong Australian bottled beer, and we had a rousing party. Vincent Dishman had unearthed an ancient gramophone together with a cracked selection of incongruous records, among the more ironically memorable of which were 'East of the Sun' and 'I Wanna Zoot Suit'. We went on drinking and singing into the early hours of the morning, acting under the influence of alcohol with the excitable nervous energy one could always summon up in those desolate desert spots. As usual the acknowledged master in these revels of ours was David Richards, now a major with the Military Cross.

Next morning, by way of penance, there was a long and dusty route march. At one halt, when we lay sprawled by the roadside with our feet in the air, the CO came past in his staff car and announced brightly, 'The brigade's going to Syria on a mountain warfare course. We leave in three days' time.' Later there was considerable speculation in the mess. Did this mean Italy?

Khanaqin, Iraq.

The move was to be by desert convoy across Transjordan and Syria to the Lebanon, a six-day trip. But when the time came, I did not travel with the others as I had to go into hospital with the unromantic malady of roundworm, and made the journey later in the week attached to a regiment of gunners who were bound for the same destination. It was pitch-black as we drove into Tripoli in the rain – an incessant, torrential downpour. After negotiating the greasy streets we slept the night inside the vehicles. By morning the sun was shining and I found the battalion in a nearby olive grove, encamped beneath the trees.

I I

It was early spring in 1944 and the scenery in Northern Lebanon was spectacular. The narrow coastal plain behind Tripoli was studded with olive and orange groves. To the west lay the Mediterranean; to the east, behind a line of conical foot-hills the mountains rose steadily towards the snow-capped crests of the Jebel Liban range, which reached a height of 10,000 feet above sea level. The contrast was dramatic: an hour's ride by jeep took one from the near-tropical warmth of the coast to freezing, wind-swept heights, along roads that wound through passes with sheer cliff-faces on either side and picturesque cascading waterfalls.

On the fringe of the hills, within walking distance of the camp, were several half-hidden villages, bright and clean, with narrow cobbled streets. The French influence was unmistakable: quiet tonsured monks, buxom peasant girls, and alert-looking schoolboys carrying satchels and wearing jerseys and short trousers. The villagers were brisk and welcoming, and it was a pleasure to be able to mix with 'locals' once again in beershops with unlimited bottled ale. There was

Royal Sussex officers in Persia. In the foreground from left to right: John Martin, John Halsall and Hugh Horsley.

no thieving in this area, and no need for sentries around the camp at night. When the children ran after you in the streets it was no longer for bully beef that they were begging but for pencils.

The course was run by the Middle East Mountain Warfare Training Centre and, apart from a few introductory lectures, consisted entirely of battalion exercises in the mountains. On exercises the role of intelligence officer was a congenial one for a subaltern: no more standing-to with the men for hours in cold slit trenches, but free movement in the battalion area and much hobnobbing with majors. The intelligence officer served as something of a handmaiden to the colonel. I always travelled in the CO's jeep, along with the driver, a signaller with a wireless set and other accoutrements, all our equipment and a profusion of maps.

Previously, John McCully had seemed a rather remote authoritarian figure; now I saw him in a more human light. He was a bundle of restless energy and animation. Though he was nearly twice my age, he could thrash me hollow on foot in the mountains, leaving me panting a hundred yards behind

129

him as I struggled along with my unwieldy mapboard. I rather fancied myself at map-reading, but he was in a different class. At odd moments in the jeep he would shade the contours of the map with rapid strokes in a spectrum of colours to give a vivid picture of the terrain ahead. He saw the world through a tactician's eyes and even on routine journeys was forever exclaiming, 'One would have to hold that ground over there . . . No. Perhaps that mountain is the key,' or 'What a wonderful headquarters that would make.' Every situation was a matter of life or death to him. He was a true professional, and he made the rest of us – detached and cynical as we affected to be – seem distinctly amateur.

In the course of a month we carried out a number of exercises over a wide area. Each one began with a vehicle convoy crawling along precipitous roads to a rendezvous in a remote mountain village. This would be followed by a long and confusing climb, generally in the dark, towards some distant objective. The rifle companies led the way, the men grunting and swearing when the going was hard; they slithered and stumbled on the slippery cliff-like faces, with a trail of doughty pack-mules lumbering behind. We normally spent three or four days of sweat and toil at a time on the mountainside in a variety of manoeuvres, with no sleep and little food, except for some stew and a mug of tea on the objective, before we heard the magic words 'exercise close'. When we got back to camp the routine was dinner, a bath, some beer and sleep, followed by two or three days of indolent recuperation before the next exercise.

We had half expected that we would go to Italy as soon as our training was completed, but instead we received orders to return to Paiforce to undertake garrison duties in Teheran. The ten-day, thousand-mile journey along the all-too-familar route passed without incident.

The camp on the outskirts of Teheran proved a comfortable one. Our main duties centred once again on a soul-destroying round of guards, this time at the Embassy, the Middle East Supply Centre, the Command Supply Depot and the Workshops. The city at the time was under joint occupation by Russian, American and British troops, all vying with each other in military pomp and ceremonial. Each morning we had an elaborate guard-mounting ritual, over which as the newly promoted adjutant I had to preside. The

Guard of honour for the Shah and Empress of Persia, Tehran, 1944.
The officer commanding the guard is Graham Jelley.

Officers' mess at Karind.

turn-out of the men was superb and the camp, a showpiece of paint and whitewash, was nicknamed 'The Cemetery' by some irreverent Americans. One of the battalion's more noteworthy assignments was to provide a guard of honour for the Shah and Empress of Persia in a ceremony held in a nearby sports stadium.

There was quite a social life, too, especially for the officers, with a round of parties inside and outside the camp; and every evening the bright lights of the town offered a tempting invitation. It was a highly civilised existence, but a long way from the war. Our only reminder of the real hostilities was a couple of large maps on the wall of the mess, one of Russia and the other of Normandy, on which we boldly plotted, with coloured tape and drawing pins, the progress of the Allied armies from daily news bulletins by the local station, 'Radio Teheran, Iran'.

One day the unexpected news arrived that the battalion was now destined for Burma. A number of minor changes in organisation were promptly made, and on the plain beyond the camp the rifle companies began to practise highly unrealistic manoeuvres, called JEWTs, or 'jungle exercises without trees'.

In September we moved to a remote and isolated station near Karind, where the camp was gritty and fly-blown and there was a fair amount of sickness. The only notable diversion during our stay was a pirated copy of *Lady Chatterley's Lover*, which was passed from tent to tent in the officers' lines. There was no further news about Burma, and after two unsatisfactory months we moved once again to Khanaqin in the plains, travelling this time on foot through the Mistletoe Pass, a rugged track over the mountains some miles south of Paitak. The hundred-mile march, which took five days, was something of an infliction after the indulgence of Teheran and the inactivity of Karind.

Life was equally uneventful at Khanaqin, and the full tedium of our two-year tour in Paiforce began to make itself felt. The flood of paper instructions from headquarters in Baghdad was reaching its zenith and we in the orderly room bore the brunt of it. The monotony of our lives was demoralising. Indeed our existence here seemed quite pointless. Somehow, life in the mess had lost its former charm. All we seemed to do was drink, gossip and criticise each other in a petty, carping way like a lot of old women. The truth was that after so long together in the confined surroundings of camp life even the best of friends became sick of the sight of each other.

By Christmas, earlier wild rumours of the likely ending of the war in Europe by the turn of the year had been abruptly silenced by the sudden German onslaught in the Ardennes. Over the holiday we listened in the comfort of the mess to wireless bulletins about the fighting in the snow around Bastogne. In one of these broadcasts the announcer urged his listeners to 'say a prayer for the infantry tonight'.

A few days later news came that the battalion would not be going to Burma after all and was unlikely ever to be used on operations again. However, four officers and fifty men were needed as reinforcements for the Central Mediterranean Force in Italy, where the Allied advance had come to a halt for the winter on a line stretching from coast to coast just north of Florence. Three officers promptly volunteered: George Blunden, the intelligence officer, Charles Freeman, the signals officer, and Henry Salter, a lieutenant from 'C' Company. The CO agreed to my joining them. There was no difficulty in finding the fifty men. Among those who elected to go was my batman, Hinkins, and also Paddy Mahon and the brothers Cobb from Ten Platoon in 'B' Company.

Our departure was fixed for a day in mid-January 1945. We were to be driven late in the evening to nearby Khanaqin station to catch the midnight train. This afforded ample time for valedictory celebrations, and when the draft was finally paraded in the car park ready to leave two-thirds of the men were irretrievably drunk. Almost the whole battalion had gathered to bid us farewell, and in the general confusion it was impossible to check individuals, or even to count heads. There was nothing for it but to shove them all into the back of the trucks, willy-nilly, with their friends still clinging to their necks in fervent alcoholic farewells.

At the station the chaos was even greater. The platform was a seething mass of khaki figures, many of them clutching bottles and with tears in their eyes, while a couple of piano accordions supplied a blaring accompaniment. To cap everything, another draft from a regiment of field gunners arrived to catch the same train. They were in an even worse condition than our men and promptly began to sing a corrupt and highly provocative version of 'Sussex by the Sea'. The railway transport officer and I were helpless. We shrugged our shoulders, and I decided to shut myself in the compartment and hope for the best. Miraculously, the train moved off on time without a single absentee.

We slept soundly through the night, reaching Baghdad in a subdued mood at dawn. There we spent a couple of days, drawing rations, NAAFI supplies, cookers, lamps and other equipment for the next stage of the move, across the Syrian desert to Palestine. An Indian transport company drove us in a convoy of troop-carrying lorries. The journey lasted four or five days, with overnight stops at rudimentary staging camps.

There was a marvellous sense of liberation in that exhilarating drive westwards across the open desert. We followed the standard drill of a halt of twenty minutes on every even hour, and fifty minutes at noon. During one morning halt we stood beside a large painted signboard which proclaimed, 'You are now leaving PAIFORCE.' A rousing cheer went up and in a fit of exuberance the men tore the notice down and hurled stones at it.

At the midday halt there was always a roaring petrol fire beside the vehicle and a welcome mug of tea with our haversack rations of cheese and dates. I sometimes found it difficult not to envy my travelling companion in the leading fifteen-hundredweight truck, a lean and patriarchal subahdar in charge of the Indian drivers, who almost instantaneously on arrival was invariably presented by his men with a vast plate of curry and chapatis. But by evening when we reached the staging area our own cooks, who were sent on ahead of the main party, would already be preparing the meal. As darkness fell the men would gather expectantly around the cookers. It was cold and windy in the desert on those early January nights, but cheerful enough by the fire. Sometimes there were a few ragged tents in the camp, sometimes not. When we struck lucky there was an hour or two of pontoon after dinner by the light of a hurricane lamp.

The road journey ended at Haifa, where we stayed overnight, leaving early next morning on a densely packed train for Alexandria. We spent a couple of days in a comfortable transit camp, in a setting of billowy white sand and scattered scraggy palms, preparing for the voyage. Then early one morning we were driven to the docks in a long line of troop carriers, and with remarkably little fuss filed aboard the

MV *Meridan*, a French ship of medium size. We left Alexandria late that night and by dawn were well out to sea on a squally Mediterranean, surrounded by humped-up, stormy black clouds and driving rain.

It was the most cosmopolitan ship in the world. The crew were French and the passengers an intriguing assortment of nationalities. Sharing the first-class deck with British and South African officers were a group of aristocratic-looking Poles accompanied by their women, a few Italians, some taciturn Yugoslavs who were members of the Special Boat Service and a handful of Greek civilians. On the lower deck were the British other ranks, travelling above sea-level, or so it was claimed, for the first time in recorded memory; below them was a large draft of sullen Cape-Coloured soldiers, commanded by white officers. Further below still was a contingent of Cypriot muleteers, swarthy little men with sad eyes, clearly hating the sea. Forward was a draft of Indian Engineers, accepting their ordeal with pasty expressions of resignation; and somewhere in the bowels of the vessel were the Basutos, bewildered creatures looking totally out of place. Altogether, a remarkable cross-section of humanity.

But the weather was no respecter of national identities, and as the day wore on it grew steadily worse. The ship lurched and rocked like a cockle-shell, and by evening half the passengers were prostrate with sea-sickness. The first-class dining room was almost deserted. Most of the men on the mess decks had either crawled under the hammock racks or lay sprawled lifelessly across the tables. The food, brought in containers from the galley, was rejected by everyone, except for a small band of dogged and insensitive stalwarts who blatantly ate their way through double rations during the whole voyage.

Next morning things were no better. Below deck there was pandemonium, with the South African officers kicking and shouting in a vain attempt to drive their troops aloft for 'Boat Stations' parade. On deck, negroes with ashen faces – somehow their condition looked so much worse behind their black colouring – were draped helplessly across the duck-boards. The OC Troops with his train of satellites toured the ship, ranting and posturing with no discernible effect. The sharp stench of vomit was everywhere and the stairs between decks were covered with slime, as if it were not already difficult enough to hold one's footing against the steep, rhythmic slither of the ship.

The lounge was sadly depleted. Only the Poles appeared unaffected. The men, smoking through long cigarette holders, were absorbed in endless games of bridge, and there were no casualties among their womenfolk. One of the women was particularly striking – a long-limbed and statuesque blonde in a pure white sheepskin coat. She was the cynosure of every glance. When one gazed at her she merely stared back in cool composure through blue, unsmiling eyes. I could not recall women quite like this back in England, but perhaps it was just that we had been away too long.

Among the Cape-Coloured soldiers on board was a small group of entertainers, and in the afternoon – notwithstanding the weather – they were prevailed upon to give a concert in the lounge. The Poles monopolised the front seats. The band began with some gentle, lilting jazz, and then the vocalist, a shy, slender negro lad, crooned in a sweet voice, tender as a woman's, 'I'll get by, as long as I've got you'. The music was an odd blend of the primitive and the sentimentally sophisticated. Two of the band came forward, one of them lanky and effeminate, the other stocky and grinning like a pygmy. They danced together, pretending to be women, wriggling their bodies in suggestive movements. It was indecent in an artless way, a performance meant for the rugged informality of an all-male canteen and out of place in this polished lounge in front of ladies. At first we felt uncomfortable, but there was no need to have worried. The Polish women did not betray a flicker of embarrassment. The beautiful one sat through it all, faintly interested but unmoved, with all the placid superiority of a countess contemplating the antics of her retainers. She brought a distinct scent of feudalism into the lounge.

A single white South African soldier was playing a guitar in the little orchestra, taking the place of a regular member who was sick. He strummed away in the background chewing gum, a vacuous and conceited-looking youth with brilliantined hair. Standing beside me in the audience was a big South African major in charge of the draft, who suddenly turned and said, 'Damned sporting of that European to play up there with those niggers!'

On the third day at sea the weather improved. It was still

rough, but brilliant sunshine had broken through the thick canopy of cloud, and the motion of the ship, though still pronounced, was less violent than before. In the late afternoon we sighted Sicily. The blanched faces had begun to disappear, and now quite a spirited crowd assembled on the boat deck to scrutinise the grim silhouette of Etna rising sheer out of the sea.

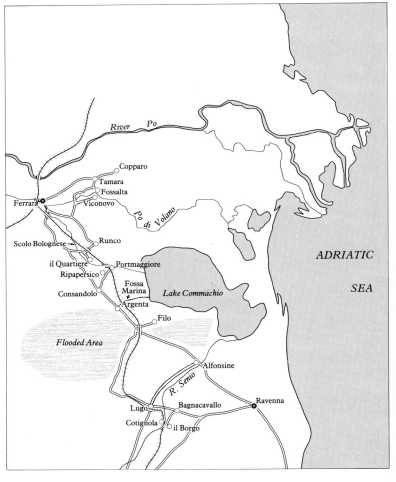

North Italy, 1945
Scale one inch = 15 miles

Part Four: Italy

12

Early next morning we sailed into Taranto harbour. Our first sight of Italy was not particularly inspiring. The docks were much like any the world over: dingy wharves, black scummy water, deserted goods wagons on a network of rails, lines of lorries with bored-looking drivers, and here and there a mournful and unhurried corporal from the movement control staff. Our draft was detailed as a baggage party, with the result that we spent the morning and most of the afternoon unloading other people's luggage from the hold. When at last the task was completed, we were driven to the transit camp, which was situated in an olive grove above the town. It was a short up-hill journey through grubby slums, with little to enliven it, except for a glimpse of an occasional crumbling wall decorated in black paint with Mussolini's old slogan, '*Vivere, Credere, Combattere*', a sad parody now of the Duce's pretensions.

Within a day or two we were on our way to Naples. We travelled by night in a typical Italian troop train – shutters instead of windows, bare wooden seats with any lingering trace of upholstery long since removed, no lights or heating – which thudded mercilessly over the uneven track with the unsprung deadness that was a feature of the Italian railway system. Fortunately we had a candle and were able to play cards, muffled in our overcoats. After we had had breakfast on the platform at Salerno, the train ran along the coast between tall craggy cliffs and the sea, which sparkled in the clear winter sunlight. Eventually Vesuvius and the bay came into view. We pulled into Naples station, which was industrious and civilised, and swarming with porters. As we searched for our vehicles outside, the transport clerk mentioned that Gigli would be singing at the Opera House at the end of the month.

Our destination was the Infantry Reinforcement and

Training Depot. This was some thirty miles inland at Cervinara, a dismal village with cobbled streets and murky shops lit by hurricane lamps which seemed to shiver beneath a wooded, snow-capped mountain range. The adjacent camp looked chill and forbidding. When we arrived the men were promptly marched away to a remote corner and separated from us completely; the officers were herded into a group of tents with scores of other officers from a miscellany of regiments. The studied brusqueness of our treatment and the calculated discomfort of the living conditions left us feeling distinctly depersonalised.

At the depot one of the many routine duties was that of orderly officer, which involved among other things visiting the Guard Room. The detention cells were crammed to overflowing, mainly with deserters from units in the north who were awaiting trial. The figures for desertions in the Italian campaign, if published, would be quite staggering. Those locked up here, the ones who had been caught, were only a fraction of the total. The rest were hiding in towns and farmsteads, and the hills – so we were told – were full of them. These were the men who would suffer anything rather than face the 'line' again. Desertion was not a matter of black and white, and never an easy option. So much depended on the amount of pressure an individual was asked to bear. For many, it had been a long campaign and a harsh winter; and for some this was the limit. A soldier who deserts does so not from simple fear of death or injury, but from a refusal of the body and spirit to face any longer the endless discomfort and racking dread, day after day. Then a sudden ungovernable reflex can drive him in desperation to flee the horror he can endure no more, regardless of the severity and ignominy of the consequences.

By contrast a VC joined us for dinner one evening in the mess. He was a big, limping Hampshireman, with piercing eyes, who had won the decoration in Italy the year before. His medal ribbon fascinated me. As a mark of esteem the Victoria Cross has a unique and timeless distinction. There is an indescribable grandeur about physical courage in a man; it is like extreme beauty in a woman, an absolute beyond criticism. No doubt there are other attributes as praiseworthy as courage, and other activities of more abiding value than war; but a soldier does not see it that way. Even the most outstanding distinctions in other walks of life – in politics, art, literature, or science – lack the direct and universal impact of the Victoria Cross. The sight of that purple ribbon on the battledress of a serving soldier seemed to put everything else in the shade.

After some two weeks at the depot we received a transfer notice for No. I Corps Reinforcement Unit near Arezzo in the north. By now, of the four officers who had left the old battalion, only two remained, George Blunden and myself. Having been rejoined by the men of the original draft, we caught the train from Caserta station at dusk. We reached Rome by mid-morning and found we had a couple of hours to kill. I took a calculated risk and let the men loose in the city. They trickled back in twos and threes, plastered with vino and in the best of humour. There was consternation at the last minute when two of them failed to appear, having earlier been seen disappearing into a brothel near the station. Perversely the train was punctual, and I was not able to hold it up. This was a mortifying blot on an otherwise unblemished record and I railed against the rest of the men, swearing never to trust them again. The train steamed away, pausing momentarily at a suburban halt a few miles up the line; there on the platform were the two absentees. The RTO had rushed them across the city at breakneck speed in a jeep, and the draft was complete once more. I no longer had it in my heart to be angry with them.

All night long the train thundered along the bumpy track to Arezzo, which was the rail terminus at that time. We were left to slumber in the coaches until daybreak. At dawn we were driven in three-tonners to the reinforcement unit, a delightful journey along a winding, cratered road through the valley of the Arno. The scenery even in the muted tints of February was wonderfully serene and varied after the harsh landscapes of the Middle East.

The camp was near the town of San Giovanni, midway between Arezzo and Florence. The men were billeted in a nearby factory building and the officers housed in tents with brick fireplaces and chimneys, which were pitched around the hutted mess. Here, the life proved to be one of masterly inactivity, with no duties of any kind for officers. We only had to sit and await the call to the Fifth Army in the mountains. It was agreeable enough in the heart of Tuscany on sunny mornings but chilly at night, when we were glad of our ramshackle and highly dangerous fireplaces.

In the mess there were the usual hangers-on, officers who seemed to spend their lives in reinforcement camps. However, they were handy mentors in the new jargon of the Central Mediterranean Force. The Germans were called 'Teds', short for *Tedeschi*, and the front line was no longer 'the blue' but the 'sharp end'. We learned from them to refer to ourselves dismissively as 'D-Day dodgers', and to adopt a self-pitying attitude towards our equipment. 'You never get anything here, old boy. All the best kit goes to North-West Europe.'

Early one morning I took to the main road and hitch-hiked to Florence for the day. Though the city had been occupied by the Allies for some months the smell of cordite still hung about the streets. All the bridges save one across the River Arno had been destroyed; only the picturesque Ponte Vecchio with its houses and open-fronted shops had been spared. The cathedral, too, with its orange dome, black and white marble façade and elegant bell-tower, was undamaged. Most of the city's portable art treasures had been stowed away in places of safety, though there was one gallery open. I was taken round by a decrepit old guide, who reeked of garlic. He was full of gossipy anecdotes of Michelangelo and Leonardo, whom he treated with patronising pride as local boys made good; through the windows he pointed out across the russet-coloured roofs and chimney pots the palace of the Medici, much as one would the residence of a wealthy but slightly discreditable neighbour.

For a while I was transported back to the Middle Ages, to the time when Florence was a dynamic and prosperous city and the Florentines dominated the world's culture with the same effortless supremacy as that with which their Roman cousins had dominated its politics more than a thousand years before. Nothing could have been a greater contrast to these glories than the sorry spectacle of Florence in 1945 and the tragic ruin of modern Italy. The country was ravaged from end to end in a disastrous war, in which the Italians themselves no longer had a part. They were left a defeated and dispirited people, mocked by the relics of former greatness.

Our own activities back at the camp were sporting rather

than artistic, our principal diversion being rugby. Equipped with borrowed shorts and ill-fitting boots, and after some practice in an adjacent field, we were rash enough to challenge a team from the South African Armoured Division. The match was played on a pony-trotting track at nearby Montevarchi, and we received somewhat cavalier treatment. On another occasion, against less formidable opposition in the handsome stadium at Arezzo, we gave a better account of ourselves. After a good muddy game and a shower we had a look around the town.

Though many of the buildings had been damaged in the fighting of the previous autumn, the rhythm of everyday life had already been resumed; the streets and main piazza were crowded with laughing townsfolk, parents with children and lovers arm-in-arm taking an early evening stroll. I think we secretly envied the Italian men, begrudging them the outward normality of their existence. The prospect of life ahead of them might be hard, but at least they were reunited with their families and friends. These unworthy sentiments were dispelled readily enough in the officers' club later, when a few rousing cognacs and vermouth soon restored our geniality and set us up for the rest of the evening. All the same, in our sing-song on the return journey to camp, after we had exhausted the standard repertoire of bawdy rugby ballads, we lingered wistfully on 'Lili Marlene', that poignant melody which captured perfectly the mood of the Italian campaign. We sang the soldiers' version:

> Please Mr Churchill,
> When do we go home?
> We conquered Napoli
> And now we've conquered Rome.
> When do we go ho-ome?
> Oh! When do we go home?

After some three weeks at San Giovanni we were un-expectedly told that we were to be switched to No.2 Corps Reinforcement Unit in the Adriatic sector, where the Eighth Army was facing the Germans entrenched along the River Senio. This involved us in a lengthy and roundabout train journey via Rome. We travelled in cattle trucks, and for most of the time rain pelted down in sheets. But we were comfortable enough inside, with the sliding doors shut tight and blankets spread out on the floor, and progress was good apart from several long inexplicable halts.

At one such stop after nightfall near a large and busy railway junction we were shunted into a siding. The driver promptly unhooked his engine and abandoned us. A few of the men clambered down from the trucks and sprinted across the lines of glinting rails towards the distant rumbling locomotives to beg for hot water to make tea; others lit petrol fires beside the track to heat their tins of stew. Meanwhile, a new engine cruised stealthily out of the darkness. After a sharp clatter of couplings, we found ourselves on the move again in a sudden unheralded departure. There was a great deal of shouting and shoving as the men piled in. They hitched their blazing brew cans to the outer doors of the wagons and, as the train gathered speed through the darkness, its sides were aglow with swinging braziers. From one of the open trucks came the strains of an accordion and a trumpet.

By morning in bright sunshine we reached Falconara, a railway junction on the Adriatic coast north of Ancona. From there the track ran northwards beside the sea-shore for thirty miles to Fano. This was a compact coastal town, with remnants of Roman walls and a scatter of mediaeval buildings, as well as a row of modern hotels skirting a sandy beach. We were gratified to find that the reinforcement unit was located in a commodious barrack block, a legacy from Mussolini.

At Fano there was even less work to do than at San Giovanni and I passed the time poring over an Italian grammar and vocabulary. I called on the Town Major to see if he knew anyone who could give me some lessons. He recommended *La Signora Bisconti*, and I sought out the lady. She lived in a lofty tenement off the gloomy back streets. The noisy American army monopolised the bottom two floors, and the signora occupied the top one. At the head of the staircase I groped my way to the end of a dark corridor and knocked on the door. From within came a quick cry of '*Avanti*'. The signora was inside, a tiny grey-haired lady with shrivelled cheeks but with bright eyes and a trim figure. She wore an apron and was busy with the household chores. I said that I wanted to learn Italian. '*S'accomodi*,' she exclaimed waving me to a chair. 'I shall probably be here only a short

while, but I should like to do as much as possible in the time,'
I explained. 'You could have two lessons a week,' she
suggested. 'Could I have two a day?' I asked. She was a bit
taken aback, but consented. 'One hour in the morning and
one in the evening.'

I began lessons with a will, seated on a stool at the kitchen
table opposite the signora. She made me read aloud from a
large copy of *I Promessi Sposi*, which had huge print like a
child's primer. She exercised all the classic tyranny of the
professional pedagogue, though she was for ever popping off
to see to the vegetables or the squalling grandchild. I felt very
sorry for her. She was clearly a person of refinement and
culture, used to far better times. Now she was living in
poverty in a dingy flat at the top of a grim tenement building,
earning a few extra lire by teaching languages. Yet she was a
proud woman, of a finer mould than most Italians, and quite
free of the over-accommodating humility of many of them.
One day she told me that her favourite language was German
and that she liked the Germans best of all. Some of them used
to come to her house. 'Such big delightful boys,' she said. Her
candour was refreshing, though I sometimes thought she
must have got the sides mixed up. It was almost as though she
had been cut off from the war. When I brought her gifts of
chocolate, soap and cigarettes, which were like gold dust to
civilians at the time, she was surprised and genuinely
embarrassed.

I made good progress with the Italian but my instruction
was cut short when posting notices at last arrived. The draft
was to be split up and allocated to various units in the 78th
Division. George Blunden was sent to the Royal West Kents,
and I was posted, as a subaltern, to the 1st East Surreys.

13

The East Surreys were in the 11th Infantry Brigade, with
the 2nd Lancashire Fusiliers and the 5th Northamptons. The
battalion, having spent the winter in the mountains of the
Northern Apennines, was now in a rest and training area in
the plains of Emilia south of Forli. When I reported to

The Forum at Rome.

headquarters, which was in a large villa four miles from Forlimpopoli, the adjutant told me I was being posted to 'A' Company and offered to run me round in a jeep.

The company was a mile or so away along a dusty side-road in the village of San Pietro in Guardiano. The officers were billeted in two adjacent farmhouses belonging to the same Italian family. Mama, the wizened old lady of the household, greeted me cordially and took me to the mess, which was in one of the front rooms. It looked quite comfortable and was furnished with some armchairs, a pile of books and a flask of Chianti. The bedrooms upstairs were all full, however, and I was told to sleep next door with the family. Mama offered to show me the room. On the way over she enquired, 'Are you captain or lieutenant?' They were sticklers for rank those Italians. '*Oggi capitano, domani tenente*,' I explained with a grin. That was too deep for her.

The house was a small detached building of plain grey stone situated close to the road. Scrawled on the wall in chalk were the words, '*Letto per ufficiale*'. The family shared the ground floor with the domestic animals. Musty sacks of flour were stacked against the whitewashed walls and there was a smell of garlic everywhere. My bedroom had a bare floor, a shuttered window, a hard mattress and a washstand. While I was looking round, the seventeen-year old daughter of the house appeared in the doorway. After a hearty shout of 'Hello *tenente!*' she introduced herself as Pina. She was not in the least shy and, pointing to the bed, declared laughingly, 'Good bed that one. It's mine.' I thanked her for the loan. She and the rest of the family – about eight in all – slept in the other two small bedrooms, though quite how they managed it I was never able to fathom.

Later, next door, I met the rest of the officers. The company commander, Major Robinson, who had had long service overseas, was on the point of returning to England under the newly-instituted leave scheme. My fellow subalterns were Ray Gates and Dennis Smith, who had both joined the battalion the previous autumn and had spent the winter months with the company in the snows of Mount Spaduro. The battalion MO, Captain Miedema, a kindly Dutch doctor, was also billeted with us. Finally, there was the company second-in-command, Captain Giles, with an MC and bar, who had been with the battalion throughout the campaign.

Teddy Giles was of medium height but most sturdily built, with a bushy moustache and a terrifically hearty manner. He would stride indoors, calling out in a voice like thunder, *'Buon giorno, Mama? Come state?'* and burst into peals of laughter that shook the house. He was the yeoman type, and blunt, almost to the point of rudeness, in speech. At our first meeting he complained, 'The CO doesn't like me – he says I'm irresponsible.' He spoke naively, like an enormous unruly child. One day we fell to talking of medals. He discussed the subject openly, answering with frankness questions about his own decorations. He was not the diffident, public school type, and had none of the conventional English mock modesty that surrounds this topic with taboos. I was interested later to watch the reactions of the men towards him. In the previous battalion one or two officers had been idolised for individual acts of bravery; but the men took Teddy Giles for granted. They were inclined to laugh at his ups and downs, for he radiated enthusiastic ideas that rarely came to fruition; his courage was so much a part of him that it was barely noticed.

The following night there was an informal dinner party in the mess. Some gunner officers were invited along with Captain Squire from 'B' Company, a particular friend of Teddy Giles, who looked like a pocket version of Teddy though he was more quietly spoken. Normally we had our own cook but in honour of our guests Mama had been specially dragooned into cooking spaghetti. The flat pasta was first rolled up like a pudding and then cut into narrow strips like streamers and served with a meat sauce. The others raved about it, but I found it rather dull. The truth is that something in the very conviviality of the occasion made me miss the old battalion more keenly than at any time since I had left, and nothing had quite the same sparkle any more. It was pretty churlish of me to feel this way towards Mama and my new companions, who could not have been more friendly; and doubly so, since no one did more than myself during the evening to help drain dry a vast wicker-covered carboy of white wine which Teddy Giles had bought in Ravenna a day or so before.

During the ensuing week there was a succession of exercises: a night attack through the vineyards behind the farmhouse, a bridging exercise across the River Montone

Ponte Vecchio, Florence, 1945.

near Forli and an assault river-crossing over one of the many canals. After this last exercise I called on my men in their billet. The men of Eight Platoon were not easy to get to know. They had had considerable battle experience and were hard, critical and grudging. They had seen plenty of officers, and could scarcely be expected to welcome a new one with open arms. It was a very different reception from the naive, friendly acceptance of the Sussex platoon.

This was supposed to be a rest period but the training was strenuous and I was glad to get back to the farmhouse for a night's rest after each day's work. On my way indoors one evening I was invited into the family living room. 'Come and join us, *tenente*,' Mama sang out, as I was about to mount the stairs. I was given a chair by the fire, where two batmen were already comfortably ensconced. Mama had a grandchild, an enormous rosy-cheeked *bambino*, who sat on the table top while she fed him with bread and milk. Mama and the *bambino* dominated the household. The daughter-in-law, the child's mother, sat demurely beside the table, a frail, pale, pretty creature in pink. She smiled sweetly, but seemed out of place in this sturdy, rustic household. Papa and the son, the child's father, stayed in the background. The latter was a mere slip of a lad. The two men sat mutely in the shadows at the back of the room, smoking silently. Were they just apathetic, I wondered, or did they feel a resentment towards us, bursting into the privacy of their domestic circle and absorbing the attention of their womenfolk?

The two batmen were firm friends of the family and they continually teased them in their jocular, dog-Italian. One of them tossed the *bambino* a lira note to play with. The child with instinctive wisdom put it on one side and asked for another. Mama scolded him and told him to hand the note back. 'Let him keep it,' shouted the batman. But Mama did not like it. Useless scrap of paper though it was, something at the back of her thrifty peasant mind recoiled at the extravagance.

Pina came in from the darkness outside. She was a stout but comely girl, with all the florid beauty of the soil. She had been in the fields with her boy-friend, a sleek, shifty-looking youth from the village. Now she had returned with flushed cheeks and a defiant look on her face. A fine lusty young peasant girl this, with a proud, independent spirit. I sometimes saw her in the mornings, washing in a bucket of icy water from the pump. There was no room indoors – for the family were packed like sardines in their bedrooms – so Pina always conducted her ablutions in the open air for all the world to see, splashing her legs and neck vigorously with cold water. She worked hard all day in the fields at the back of the house, but the evenings were her own. Whenever she cycled down the road she always waved gaily to all the troops she passed on the way. Officers, sergeants, privates – they were all the same to her. She knew well enough why they all stared after her and she revelled in it.

Pina took her place on the stool by the fire between the two batmen. In the low raftered room the family chattered away, regaling each other with references to the hardships and horrors of the occupation. They pulled solemn faces and made suitably dramatic gestures at any mention of the infamous *Tedeschi*. How quickly the Italians had changed sides. Somehow their colourful and exaggerated tales never quite rang true.

About a week after my joining the unit, the buzz went round that we would be moving within a matter of days. The men had become remarkably well-integrated into the life of the village during their two months stay, and they pressed for a suitable farewell party. A dance, perhaps? This suggestion was adopted on the colour-sergeant's assurance that the girls would turn up as long as we supplied enough food. I was deputed to organise the music. There were one or two instruments in the company, but no piano. I sought help from the battalion padre. After some initial hesitation, he conceded that there was a well-to-do family in a villa near headquarters whom he might persuade to lend me their piano, provided I promised solemnly to return it in perfect condition. I gave him my word, looking him straight in the eye as I did so, for he was a muscular Irishman with the MC, and not a man to be trifled with, despite his cloth.

I was delayed for an hour or so on the evening of the dance and when I reached the small wooden hall near the church the noise was already echoing down the street. Inside, the din was deafening. One or two Italian girls, more brazen than the rest, danced with soldiers; and a couple of drunken troops tottered around the room, arms clasped about each other's waists. The rest of the men stood in grinning groups, with great mugs of vino in their hands. The band was performing quite well in the circumstances, but the piano had the tinny harp-like sound that one associated with church halls in England. The men had removed the top and front of the instrument to increase the volume, and a bunch of them were clustered round the pianist, arms draped over each other's shoulders, hair dishevelled, faces flushed, singing in tuneless, incoherent voices. The vino was dripping on to the keyboard and seeping inside. I was horrified, but it was too late to do anything. I couldn't bear to watch any longer. I buried myself for the rest of the evening in a small back room. Wine flowed over the floor and lapped around the pile of empty ammunition tins which served as a bar.

Next morning we all had hangovers. Then there was the question of the piano. An early visit of inspection to the hall showed that the keys were yellow with stale vino and that not a single note would sound. I was in something of a panic. One of the lance-corporals suggested that we sought the help of the village carpenter, who was also a piano tuner. A message to the old man elicited a promise that he would come as soon as he could.

By midday the carpenter had still not turned up so the corporal and I called at his workshop. A small, shy man, he was busy making a coffin for one of the village children who had just died, beating it out of old petrol tins. 'We must finish this job first, it is so unhealthy otherwise,' he explained apologetically. At last he was ready to join us in the hall. By heroic efforts he succeeded in an hour or two in making all but three of the notes strike, before he finally exclaimed, '*Finito!*' We gave the woodwork of the piano a generous measure of spit and polish, bundled it into a truck and with a silent prayer sent it back to the owner. I vowed never to borrow another piano as long as I lived.

Later that afternoon all the officers were summoned to battalion headquarters for a conference on the forthcoming move. The chairs were arranged round a blackboard on the lawn. I asked Teddy Giles what it would be all about. 'The same old rubbish,' he said. 'Don't forget your map-boards – or something equally stupid!' However, to do the CO, Colonel Hunter, justice he gave a bright and informative account of life in the line. The River Senio was not much more than a canal, he explained, but there were steep floodbanks on each side. The Allied positions had been dug into one bank and those of the Germans into the other. In places there was no more than twenty or thirty yards between them. Both sides sat tight and were quiet by day, but at night when the rations came forward grenade-throwing began with a vengeance, and even flaming petrol tins were hurled across the water. Actual raids, though, were rare, for the tops of the banks were thoroughly mined.

Next day arrangements were made for a preliminary reconnaissance of our positions on the ground by two officers and two sergeants from each company. I went along in a jeep with our new company commander, Major Reed. We took the main road as far as Forli and then a secondary road northwards towards the front. The going was rough and dry and we were caught in the stream of dust from the leading trucks and soon smothered in thick grey grit. One of the other jeeps belonged to the Recruit Company and contained Teddy Giles, now transferred there, and the company commander, Major Jake Saunders. These two mountains of men, bulging out of the sides of the vehicle, were an amazing sight in their dusty goggles and floppy berets. As they overtook us they bawled out, 'Where are those damned Krauts?'

In the district of Romagna the land was cultivated and flat, but intersected by narrow rivers and canals, each with steep banks constructed over the centuries for purposes of irrigation and flood control. The nature of the terrain had made progress slow in this sector since each waterway was a tank obstacle and offered a potential line of defence. Nearer the front the Italians had been cleared from the area. Here and there on the roadside were minefields and ammunition dumps, but it was quiet and there was little overt evidence of activity. The highly polished guns were carefully camouflaged, and the transport was efficiently dispersed and parcelled out between the farmhouses. Notices were dotted about, 'Speed limit 10 mph. Drive slowly. *You* raise dust; *we* get shelled.'

Brigade headquarters was in a house screened by tall trees, a bleak, bare building, curiously peaceful. A solitary German prisoner was being interrogated outside and a couple of signallers in shirt-sleeves were having a belated breakfast. Suddenly a 25-pounder gun opened up from a concealed position close behind. This unexpected row gave me a shock.

I had been away from the front too long. The shells exploded with a crumping thud in the far distance. Occasionally through the stillness of the morning drifted the characteristically hollow cracking sound of grenades bursting near water and once we heard the slow, lazy popping of a tommy-gun, faint and harmless sounding, like a toy.

We were to relieve the 56th Recce Regiment, and we drove forward to their headquarters, which was in a village called il Borgo. Though the land was flat, the rows of trees and vines were high enough to enable us to drive safely down the road as far as the regimental aid post. From there we had to proceed on foot to the company headquarters, for parts of the path were visible to the enemy. We ran down a ditch and dashed one by one across the lateral road. Here, one could sense the peculiar, heavy silence of the front line, that unearthly quiet that brooded over no man's land in the intervals between the fighting.

Company headquarters was in a large farmhouse with massive stone walls and a solid, timeless aspect, though pitted and scarred by shell splinters. The fir trees outside were blasted like skeletons, and the earth was pock-marked with shell holes. The troops were resting in the rear rooms and cookers were alight in the hall. In the room which served as the command post there was a divan, a few tattered easy chairs, and a table heaped with a profusion of wireless sets, message pads, codes, vino and half-eaten haversack rations. We discussed with the relaxed-looking officers of the outgoing unit the relief which was to take place next day. We were then given a quick tour of the building. Upstairs, from an artillery observation post in the skylight, our hosts with patronising casualness pointed out the forward platoon positions and the landmarks on the enemy side across the river, including the roof-tops of the town of Cotignola. 'We're really sorry to leave the line,' they said. 'It's been so peaceful and pleasant here.'

We drove back to the battalion in the late afternoon to spend our last night in the village. As I was entering the farmhouse I bumped into Papa. The old man looked grave and muttered in a solemn, reluctant voice, *'Fronte domani. Non e buono, eh?'* 'Nothing!' I said, laughingly. 'It's very quiet there now.' He looked at me, certain I must be joking. Then his face broke into a slow sad smile, but his eyes bore a pained expression, characteristic of Italians whenever the front was mentioned, reflecting an acute awareness of war as an outrage against the individual. They always seemed so much more sensitive than other races to its brutality and futility.

We moved off in convoy at dawn. The whole village had turned out to wish us God-speed and the air was full of tearful farewells. We made good time along the main road, halting for breakfast in the region of brigade headquarters. The rest of the journey was to be made on foot. The morning was sunny and the men were in good spirits. I overheard a corporal saying to some of them, 'The line's so quiet where we're going, the mobile laundry's taking over in a week's time.' As we approached the front, however, there was an unusual amount of noise: guns and mortars were firing all around and everyone seemed to be diving for cover. We took shelter ourselves until the din abated and then hurried forward. The road in front of company headquarters was scarred with smoking shell-craters; the house itself had been struck and the chimney knocked flat.

Inside, the troops were standing-to in their alarm positions and there was a considerable flap in the command post. Gone completely was the sang-froid of the day before. Instead, amid chattering wireless sets and buzzing field telephones, agitated officers were dashing to and fro. Fighting had unexpectedly flared up on the floodbank. A German patrol had crossed the river under cover of a smoke screen and attacked the forward trenches that 'D' Company would be taking over. As the smoke began to clear we could hear a running commentary from the observation post upstairs: 'The stretcher-bearers are milling around now in the platoon position. Both sides are mixed up together ... Yes, the Germans are taking the wounded prisoners back over the floodbank with them.' Gradually the hubbub subsided, and eventually the relief was completed without further incident.

The company soon settled down in the new location. There was a railway line running northwards close beside us; where it crossed the river the Germans had destroyed the bridge and established a strongpoint on both banks. Our positions, unlike those of the other rifle companies further downstream, were not in the floodbank itself but in three separate houses ranged in a semi-circle around the area of the demolished bridge. Eight Platoon was in reserve, sharing the farmhouse

'A' Company HQ, 1st East Surreys, on the River Senio, April 1945. Major John Reed, the company commander, is third from the left.

with company headquarters.

By night we had to provide a small standing patrol at 'Blow', a forward alarm post on the railway embankment about a hundred and fifty yards from the enemy. The line had been blown at this point and a small sandbag emplacement dug into the soft mud between the twisted metal rails. As soon as it was dark I crept along the foot of the embankment with a section of men. When they were in position for the night I ran through the instructions in hurried whispers with the lance-corporal and concluded in the usual way with, 'Any questions?' With a grave face he asked, 'What time is the first train?'

A day or two later we changed places with one of the other platoons, moving to a farmhouse on the right some two hundred yards further forward. This was a long, low, pink building, dignified with the name of la Palazza. It was old and plain but powerfully constructed. The garden was overgrown as a result of the neglect of the previous winter; but now, in early spring, the fruit trees in the orchard were covered with pink blossom and the grass in the fields was fresh and green and decked with gaudy weeds.

The walls of the house were sandbagged and the windows

barricaded with wardrobes and chests of drawers stuffed with pebbles and sand. Brens on fixed lines peeped through loopholes upstairs, carefully curtained with camouflaged hessian. Above us a keen-footed sniper from the intelligence section tip-toed precariously along the rafters and our sentries kept constant watch over the floodbank through a crevice in the slates. The rest of us made ourselves comfortable downstairs. The attics of these Italian houses always abounded in mattresses and we helped ourselves. We built roaring fires through incredible feats of vandalism. Nothing was sacred: precious furniture, family heirlooms and gilded picture frames were split with a bayonet and cast into the flames. We had our own cooker and were lucky enough to find several barrels of coarse vino in a cellar.

The Germans had become somewhat subdued by this stage of the war. They were desperately short of artillery ammunition, what they had being kept for emergencies. Our own gunners, on the other hand, had a remarkable surfeit of shells. All day long their guns played in an almost dilettante fashion upon the enemy positions, sending rippling salvos thudding to earth just beyond the floodbank. From time to time the Bofors guns joined in and the heavy machine-gun teams sprayed tracer down the railway embankment towards Cotignola.

We in the farmhouse were less assertive. In fact, we did not trouble the enemy more than we were morally obliged to do. There was a large stack of 2-inch mortar ammunition in the garden, which we were expected to fire each morning, and we pumped the bombs across the floodbank but without much conviction. One day we were supplied with a box of special propaganda bombs. The first few rounds burst over the enemy lines, scattering a host of white leaflets in an impressive shower. Unfortunately a perverse wind blew them back to our own lines. We found them very interesting. They pointed out in German to the enemy troops the hopelessness of their army's plight, urged them to surrender and offered a safe conduct if they would bring these dockets with them.

One night I was detailed for a reconnaissance patrol. Brigade headquarters wanted to know whether the Casa Catania di Sopra was occupied. This was a farm in front of our position, a battered group of white buildings set against the floodbank. It was a sinister place and we watched it closely from our observation post. We measured the distance, studied the air photos and took bearings. I set out that evening with Sergeant Shearer, the platoon sergeant, and Private Webb. A storm was raging and the rain – the classical accompaniment of all night patrols – poured down in torrents. But rain, at least, meant darkness. We travelled light – just overcoats and tommy-guns – with spare magazines stuffed in our pockets.

We picked our way to the company outpost, a small sandbag emplacement in an open field, then turned north through the soaking grass. Fortunately we were able to move fast, for the ground was flat and intersected with rows of vines and in the poor light we were hidden from the front. We lay down on the soaking ground, and listened. There was not a sound. Ahead I could just make out the dim silhouette of the casa. We crept forward to the next row of vines. There was now only a hundred yards to go, and I whispered to Webb to stay there and cover our move.

Tentatively, Shearer and I edged across the sodden turf. The rain continued to beat down, and water dripped from our overcoats and weapons. Overhead, our artillery were playing a fine game, sending shimmering crumps into the floodbank immediately in front of us. We inched our way towards a small haystack on a flank. Here we lay down again and listened. There was still no sound from the farmhouse. It looked safe enough, but one could never be sure. I stepped quickly round the haystack and moved forward with my finger on the trigger.

I found myself in a tiled yard with buildings on three sides. I tip-toed from one to the other. They were all empty. The casa was little better than a heap of rubble. A slit trench had been cut obliquely into the bank at the rear but there was no one in the ruins of the house. I backed cautiously towards Sergeant Shearer, fearful of stepping on a *Schu* mine. I was half-way across the yard when a Spandau snickered out from the floodbank almost above our heads. I fell flat on my face in the mud and stared forward, my heart thumping. I waited but there was no more firing. They had not been aiming at me. With relief I rose and hurried over to Shearer. 'Are you OK?' he whispered. 'Yes'. 'I thought you'd been hit when I saw you drop,' he added. Together we moved back to the phlegmatic Webb, whose eyes were scouring the darkness ahead of him.

Then we all trudged back to safety.

We arrived at company headquarters drenched and plastered with mud. The company commander questioned me over and over again. Then at last he was finished. 'Take off your boots,' he said. 'You can sleep here in the back room until morning.'

14

A few days later there was an unexpected interlude. At short notice I was chosen for a tactical training course at the divisional school near Florence. Early one Sunday morning I made the journey westwards across the Apennines from Forli in a fifteen-hundredweight truck. It was a slow, tortuous climb to the summit. We brewed tea on the windy heights overlooking the plains of Tuscany, before making the steep descent towards Florence.

The school was set in a large mansion in a valley about ten miles from the city. The surrounding hills were alive with the bright green foliage of early April and the grounds of the school were resplendent with trusses of soft blue lilac blossom. We had some delightful walks in the neighbourhood each evening. In a nearby village there was a fascinating old church with a quiet, sequestered graveyard, shaded by deep green cypresses. This had a plot for soldiers' graves, the random dead of the autumn before. Germans and British were mingled indiscriminately together, buried side by side as they had fallen. The tiny crosses were irregular and unprofessional, forlornly conveying the loneliness of the soldier killed on foreign soil. How much more beautiful they seemed than the monotonous precision of those hideous mass cemeteries of the 1914–18 war! I hoped that if I were to die in action, I would be buried in a spot like this.

The first week of the course proved unexciting but Saturday was free and the leave truck took us to Florence. There I bumped into Wally Ledger, a cheerful officer from 'D' Company. While we were drinking in a bar, one of the instructors from the course came in and, touching me on the shoulder, said quietly, 'Make it a good party boys. The course is disbanding tomorrow, and we all go back to our units. The push is starting any day now.' I had arranged to visit Dante's birthplace that afternoon; but to my shame I allowed the 'Luciola' to take precedence. This was an underground club where you could dance and drink through the afternoon and evening. How thoroughly the two of us enjoyed our last fling in Florence, and how full of braggadocio those brandies made us! By closing time we were ready to take on the whole German army by ourselves.

I returned to the unit next day, 9 April. At rear echelon there was a hold-up. The attack was due to start at seven in the evening, and no vehicles were allowed to move further forward until the opening barrage had begun. This meant kicking our heels for a couple of hours, so I took a short walk around the area. A battery of field gunners had dug in and camouflaged their guns at a cross-roads. The men in their shirt-sleeves were grinning as they polished a stack of ammunition. They were working industriously and clearly relished the prospect of pumping 25-pound shells into the enemy. Who wouldn't – from four miles away? I wondered whether any infantryman on his way into battle had ever passed gunners without envying them the comparative security and impersonality of their role. In war one grudged anyone else a task which was a fraction safer than one's own. In my own platoon one of the section commanders always referred to platoon headquarters as 'base wallahs' because they moved into the attack about fifty yards behind the leading sections. Such was the psychology of the infantryman.

As zero hour approached hordes of aircraft began dive-bombing and machine-gunning the front ahead as a prelude to the assault. The 78th Division was not taking part in the initial river crossing. The New Zealand Division was making a bridgehead just west of our positions and the 10th Indian Division was to cross a couple of miles to the east. We were to be involved in the next phase of the operation – the break-out of the Eighth Army into the Po Valley.

At length the signal was given to move forward and rejoin the battalion. After reporting briefly to John Reed at company headquarters I sought out the platoon in the pink farmhouse. They were standing-to under cover, with no active role. When I visited the sentries outside there was a terrific hullabaloo. Our artillery was keeping up an unrelent-ing barrage with the drenching superfluity of din that characterised a big offensive. The German counter-battery was active and there were shell-bursts around the house and in the orchards behind. It was no night to be abroad. Indoors we enjoyed a sense of safety in the midst of the violence. When the signal to stand down was given we sat around the fire, smoking interminable pipes and listening to a telephone commentary on the battle from the forward outposts.

Next morning the line was quiet. The initial assault had been completely successful and the tide of war had passed right away from us. By midday it was safe enough to stroll forward to the floodbank and join Ray Gates and his platoon, who had established themselves there a few nights pre-viously, through an enterprising operation with the whimsi-cal code-name of 'Pearly'. We roamed freely around where the day before we would have had to exercise great caution, and explored with interest the enemy positions near the demolished railway bridge. But we kept to well-defined tracks for a little further along the bank a man from the neighbouring platoon had had his foot blown off by a mine. Then orders came to pack up and crate all the ammunition which was lying around in profusion, and we piled the boxes into heaps to await collection.

The Italians with their instinctive intelligence soon scented the change and began to return in twos and threes to await the departure of the troops and reclaim their property. A little girl came to the pink house. She was thin and pale in a shabby black frock, about fifteen years old, but with an immature figure. She asked timidly, 'Can I have a look around my house? I want to see how much it is damaged.' I took her from room to room. She was a delicate creature and seemed completely out-of-place among these rough soldiers, who sprawled in the hay in the bedrooms playing cards and making crude jokes as she passed. She seemed relieved to find so much of the house still standing and thanked me graciously. When I thought of all our vandalism I was thoroughly ashamed. As she left, she noticed a strip of dirty web equipment lying in the garden mud. 'Can I have it, please?' she asked. 'Certainly.' It was a useless scrap of webbing. 'But what good is it?' '*Per le scarpe*,' she explained. She wanted to mend shoes with it.

Men of the 1st East Surreys entering Cotignola.

A day or two later we marched to a field near battalion headquarters and were told something of the progress of the offensive and future plans. The following morning we were driven to Bagnacavallo, and then west to Lugo. After a night's sleep in the open we took the road along the north bank of the Senio to Alfonsine, and then northwards again towards Argenta. The road had been cratered by bombs and was cluttered with the usual erratic stream of vehicles, even including some lorry loads of Italian 'co-operators'. Eventually we met our guides, who led us to a new assembly area in a huge open field.

The divisional objective was the town of Argenta, situated on a narrow stretch of solid land between Lake Commachio to the east and a waterlogged area to the west. Each spring the melting snows from the Appenines filled the irrigation channels in the plain and the Germans had deftly diverted the flood waters to turn most of the land into an impassable swamp. Our only way ahead was through the Argenta Gap. It was an obvious point of enemy resistance and this was where the next bout of fighting was expected.

The axis of advance was along the main road, but the

brigade was exploiting an unexpected penetration by the Queen's Brigade nearer to Commachio. The platoon commanders were called forward for a reconnaissance by jeep along a narrow diversionary track close to the lake. We drove for miles between flooded fields before breaking out into open farmland beyond. Near our rendezvous we spotted the brigadier in a field issuing orders to his battalion commanders.

A message arrived for us to double up in the jeeps; the company commander and one officer from each company were to go forward to the village of Filo. John Reed and I were joined in our jeep by Teddy Giles, who had taken over command of the Recruit Company, now renamed No.4 Company, and Lieutenant 'Chips' Louis. Chips was a rugged forty-year-old, and something of a living legend in the battalion. In civilian life he had been a lumberjack among other things, and had travelled all over the world. Now a veteran platoon commander, he had been continuously in action through North Africa, Sicily and Italy, and had been wounded several times.

Filo was quiet and completely deserted. The inhabitants had fled to the *rifugio*, their air raid shelter in the fields, as they had learned to do when they sensed the approach of fighting. To judge from its appearance, the village had been the scene of a vicious local action in the last twenty-four hours. The road had been ripped up by aerial bombing; the front gardens pitted with shell-bursts; the house walls punctured with tank shells; and the roofs and windows riddled with small-arms fire. 'It's been liberated,' as Chips Louis remarked. Yet these small isolated villages were a sorry sight. Caught unawares by the capricious tide of battle, they seemed so much more outraged than the devastated ruins of bigger towns and cities.

We made a quick reconnaissance of the village, decided where to put the platoons on arrival and prepared to return to the battalion. Teddy Giles had collected a chicken; it was squawking and fluttering in the bottom of the jeep. 'Don't you know how to kill it?' asked one of the other company commanders. Grabbing hold of the bird, he gave the neck a quick twist and the head came away in his hands. The decapitated fowl continued to flap about in the bottom of the car.

Chips and I squeezed ourselves into the back seat. It was

turning cold as darkness closed around us. There was spasmodic shelling and one shell exploded close to the truck with a blinding vermilion flash. 'That's all you see of the one that gets you,' was Chips's laconic comment. There were some long hold-ups in a traffic jam and it was nearly midnight when we rejoined the battalion, even though we took short-cuts. After a few hours' restless sleep on gas capes with our packs as pillows, we were roused well before dawn for the move forward to Filo.

The route was shorter and more direct than the one used earlier for the reconnaissance and we reached our destination at dawn. I led the platoon quickly into the building allotted to us, a semi-detached house on the side of the main village street. The men spent their time looting and foraging in every drawer and cupboard. Parsons produced an Italian officer's cap; and very handsome he looked in it. Others found gaudy pink material to use as neckerchiefs beneath their battledress collars. Webb patiently shadowed a chicken around the back gardens, waiting for it to lay. The clumsy ritual of smashing and looting, pointless though it was, was understandable. It was the expression of an atavistic urge which stirred in each of us, a sudden freedom from generations of repressive respect for private property. We had been reared on the gospel of 'don't touch this', and 'don't do that'; now we had a triumphant release from the cramping restraints of civilised conduct.

I was summoned to company headquarters, which was in the kitchen of one of the houses, to wait for orders. The other platoon commanders were already there. We waited and waited. At battalion headquarters the company commanders were similarly waiting; no doubt all along the line everyone was doing much the same. Our small talk was soon exhausted and we sought unsuccessfully to get some sleep on the bare tiled floor. At last the company commander returned. The battalion was to attack the southern fringe of the town of Argenta. Two companies were assaulting on the right; the job of 'A' Company was to line the railway embankment in front and give supporting fire from the left. It was always a relief to be given a specific task, and this one sounded fairly innocuous.

We moved off, section by section, through the village. In the roadway on the outskirts lay a dead German and a couple of horses, with stiff carcasses swollen like enormous football bladders. Suddenly a message came from the rear, 'About turn, and march back to the village.' We were nonplussed. The colonel was standing at the cross-roads. As we passed he called out, 'The attack is cancelled. The whole corps plan has been changed.' We returned to our previous posts, back to more hours of aimless and anxious waiting in that poky kitchen.

In the late afternoon the platoon commanders were called forward once more. The jeep took us northwards away from the village. The line of advance had shifted and we were now to by-pass Argenta, advancing across the open land to the east of the town. We drove through the forward positions of the Queen's, who had penetrated this far. The troops were standing-to in newly-dug slits. It was recently captured ground; here and there were freshly turned graves, each with an upturned rifle and a helmet – the soldier's monument. Our objectives were pointed out to us, and in the gathering dusk we drove back to Filo to pick up the men. We moved out on foot, tramping forward to the assembly area under cover of darkness. Fresh news was waiting for us: patrols from the Queen's had found all our objectives unoccupied, and the planned attack was unnecessary.

Our new orders were to resume the advance along the road. But after a few hundred yards we were halted and a message was passed down the line, 'Don't go off the road; the verges are mined.' We gazed longingly at the sodden safety of the ditch, but had no option but to sprawl in the open.

Next morning we moved to a *rifugio* in the garden of a bombed house and were able to sleep undisturbed until noon. The company commander meanwhile had gone forward to the colonel's 'order group' and in the afternoon he summoned us to join him at a forward rendezvous.

We pushed our way through the troops already on the ground. Occasionally one of them would shout a greeting as he recognised a friend; but for the most part they were detached and incurious, each one relieved at having completed his own particular task and safe in the security of his slit trench. A guide met us and led us cautiously forward along a thick hedgerow in the lee of a large farm building. I found the company commander in a front room with the officers of 'D' Company. This house had been their objective.

Wally Ledger hailed me and proffered a glass of vino, but it was not the moment to do it justice. 'There's not much time,' said John Reed, 'We're attacking in twelve minutes.' He quickly outlined the plan. Five hundred yards in front were two houses: the right-hand one was to be mine and the left Nine Platoon's. A road ran across our front immediately beyond the two houses; the company was to dig in along the line of this road. No.4 Company would be carrying out a similar task over to the left nearer Argenta, which was concealed from us by a belt of trees. Two hundred yards beyond the road was a heavily defended canal, the Fossa Marina. We were to secure the road so that the Lancashire Fusiliers could pass through after dark and seize a bridgehead.

The task was clear-cut, but everything depended on whether the houses were held by the enemy. 'Do you want artillery support?' asked the company commander. 'No,' I replied. 'We'll look after ourselves.' The field in front was decked with ominous mine notices, '*Achtung minen!*' and the skull and cross-bones sign. I had a detector, a long slender metal spike with a wooden handle; but there would be little opportunity to use it. It was one mad rush to call together the three section commanders, Corporals Butcher and Adams, and Lance-Corporal True, to point out the objective and to marshal the rest of the platoon. Then we were off into the open, the platoon deployed in extended order, one section ready to drop and give covering fire if there was trouble. We crossed the field at the double; there was no opposition. We could hear a good deal of firing among the trees nearer Argenta. The Spandaus were cracking continuously, interspersed with the pumping chatter of the Brens. But we were all right and, with a run and a bound, we were on our objective, with one section clearing the house and the rest of us digging like fury into the bank of the ditch on the roadside.

I felt light-hearted and jubilant. There was nothing to it after all! I called up John Reed on the 38 set. He was curt and brief, 'Get out of the house, dig in the ditch and keep under cover.' No.4 Company had not yet taken their objective and had already lost several men. What is more, the RAF fighter-bombers were shortly to strafe the canal line, and it was unwise to remain in a building so close while this was going on. We concentrated on digging our slits, and soon the fighter-bombers appeared overhead and swooped along the canal, blasting the canal bank a couple of hundred yards away. They were remarkably accurate and strafed the enemy for a good half hour.

Across the road to our left was a thicket of trees, which stretched to the canal. The Lancashire Fusiliers were to advance through this as soon as it was dark, and their forward troops were already beginning to assemble in the ditch alongside us. I decided to pay a call on the company commander. On the way over I came upon a platoon crouching beneath the bank. One of the men had been hit in the leg by a machine-gun bullet and was being bandaged by his friends. Further along I bumped into one of their officers whom I recognised as having been on the staff at the 'school' in Florence. He seemed more than reasonably nervous and I couldn't forbear to ask him, 'How about winning the fire-fight now, old chap?'

I was feeling jaunty as I bounced into company headquarters, which was established in a solidly-built barn. The occupants were sitting on the floor in total darkness. At first I couldn't make out who was there but after a moment or two I identified Teddy Giles and Chips as well as John Reed. Giles wanted to use the wireless – his own was broken – and to borrow stretcher-bearers to evacuate his wounded. 'Fetch starlight contraption,' he began booming over the set. His voice was loud but unemotional. A runner came in. 'One of the lance-corporals has had his foot blown off by a mine. He's still out there, sir.' 'Is no one getting him in?' Giles asked testily. 'I'll go,' grunted Chips, and he moved off without another word into the night. Another runner arrived and reported that company headquarters had had a direct hit and that several of the men were hurt. 'Christ!' muttered Teddy in a tone of resignation, and he too left the barn.

Teddy Giles and Chips Louis were two of the bravest officers in the battalion. Yet there were no heroics. There seldom were among the truly brave. To these two the aim of an attack was always straightforward enough – to take your objective and get your wounded out. Their courage lay in the determination and single-mindedness they brought to these tasks. The personal poses and banter were kept for later.

There was a sapper officer in the barn, who had been given the job of building a temporary bridge across the canal for tanks as soon as the first of the infantry were over. He was waiting to be called forward. By now the Lancashire Fusiliers had launched their attack. The thicket in front was being heavily shelled and there were noisy exchanges of small-arms fire. I did not envy the sapper his assignment. I walked back to the platoon considerably chastened and thankful for my comparative immunity from all the beastliness of this particular night's operations. I lay down in the straw in the slit trench beside my new batman, Smart, and we covered ourselves with gas capes; but it was a clammy, uncomfortable bed, for the water oozed into the trenches to a depth of several inches.

By dawn the Germans had grasped the full significance of the night's events, and every form of fire seemed to be concentrated on the forward salient in a prolonged and frightening bombardment. A few shells rained down along the road in front of us but we kept our heads down – all except Webb, who leaned over the top of the ditch and gazed endlessly through field glasses at the falling shells, seemingly fascinated.

Things were quieter at midday. Fresh troops began to pass through the bridgehead. We were told to occupy the house by the roadside. After digging alarm-trenches and posting sentries, we repaired inside to seek what comfort could be found. The farmhouse was more than usually spartan; the inhabitants had judiciously removed their furniture. However, we brought armfuls of straw from a barn and stretched out on the stone floor.

In the afternoon more troops arrived from the Irish Brigade, and tanks with flame-throwers passed through the bridgehead to clear the ground immediately to our front. Sections of infantry followed close behind to prise the enemy out of his positions. The flame-throwers swept the area with horrible effectiveness, leaving a trail of blazing houses and blackened haystacks, and the countryside was filled with billowing smoke. Though we had been unmolested all morning a surprising number of Germans emerged from the scattered buildings and trenches in front of us to give themselves up.

We watched progress from an upstairs window in the farmhouse. When the supporting infantry drew level with our house, one of them, unsure of his direction, looked across at us suspiciously and opened fire. There was a rush of wind, a click, and a lump of plaster tumbled to the floor behind us. We ducked and ran downstairs. I rushed outside waving a steel helmet. At length an officer called off the idiot, who went on his way looking most disappointed.

Next morning columns of tanks and lorry-loads of infantry surged through our positions. The offensive was going with a swing and the leading troops were by now well clear of the Argenta Gap. Some gunners arrived, charming and gentlemanly as always. They wanted half the house for a command post. The men were unanimously against granting the request. 'We captured the bloody house, why should they take it from us?' But with their customary persuasiveness the gunners talked us into it, and we divided the house in two. Later the sappers turned up to clear the road, unearthing a number of villainous-looking black anti-tank mines. Then, wonder of wonders, it was announced that a mobile cinema show was to be held in Argenta, and we were invited to send a party of men. They were given lifts into town on carriers. But when they came back they told of the damage and the carnage in the town, the shattered houses, the heaps of rubble and the mutilated bodies of Italian civilians lying in the roadway.

15

At company headquarters later in the evening fresh orders were issued. The division was now striking northwards towards the River Po. The battalion was to move forward during the night to the town of Consandolo, and from there resume the advance along the main road towards the Scolo Bolognese, a canal running westwards from Portomaggiore, where stiff resistance was expected. 'A' Company would be in the van, with Eight Platoon leading.

In the early hours we tumbled out of our straw beds and made as usual for company headquarters and the waiting lorries. In the blackness the road was full of shadowy figures. The men were busy struggling into their equipment, coughing and shivering as they loaded their weapons into the trucks. Then they climbed ponderously aboard, cursing their mates for not moving quickly enough. Soon the convoy moved off through the darkness, bumping along the bombed and unfamiliar road. I sat in the cabin with the driver, perched uncomfortably on the high seat: my pack cut into my shoulders and prevented me from leaning back; the water bottle chafed my side when I moved; and piled awkwardly between my legs were a steel helmet, tommy-gun, map case and binoculars, the inevitable impedimenta of the platoon commander. I strained hard by the glimmer of torchlight to follow the route on the map, and even harder to keep the vehicle in front in sight. No lights were allowed, apart from a minute rear lamp on each truck, and the progress of the dim red dot was most elusive. The outline of the moving truck ahead was indistinguishable except when the occasional flicker of an illicit cigarette illuminated for a second the square silhouette of the vehicle and the faces of its huddled occupants.

We reached Consandolo at dawn. Troops were standing-to in the doorways, looking drawn and weary. At the northern outskirts of the town we dismounted and took cover in some houses by the roadside. John Reed pointed along the road: 'Be ready to resume the advance, as soon as you are given the OK.' We waited patiently all day but no order came. The houses nearby had suffered the customary treatment – aerial bombardment, solid tank shot, artillery fire and a peppering with small arms. Inside, the men entertained themselves with the familiar round of looting. At intervals batches of prisoners passed down the road, the usual impassive youthful-looking Germans. Once an armoured regiment thundered towards the front, the enormous tanks tearing deep furrows in the tarred roadway. The prisoners looked up, bewildered and dazed by the sight. Our men cheered, wondering why on earth the armour didn't roll on and finish the war by themselves.

The word went round that we would not now have to advance along the road; instead the battalion was expected to make an assault crossing of the canal. The platoon commanders were summoned. We took a narrow track across land that was flat and agricultural, partly ploughed, partly pasture, and criss-crossed by vines and espalier fruit trees. Our rendezvous was a solitary farmhouse, scarred and blackened from the fighting. The farmhouses were always the selected targets, and their charred and battered shells stretched in a

A roadside rest for infantry and tanks, above.

Eighth Army troops in the final advance towards the River Po, below.

melancholy procession across the countryside, marking the route of the offensive.

We sat down by a farmyard pond. Some German prisoners were collected here for interrogation. They had been permitted to wash in the pond, and had taken off their clothes and were bathing their tired, dirty limbs in the cold, clear water, as though they were washing the war away. For them it was all over, and one could see the relief in their faces.

The company commanders returned with news that the canal had already been crossed. A company of the Irish Brigade was over and holding on. The Lancashire Fusiliers were to widen the bridgehead, and we were to follow and resume the advance next day. We were driven back to pick up the rest of the company. As I walked across to the platoon Parsons called out, 'What's the griff, sir? Is it grim?' I told the men what I knew.

Once again we took to the trucks for another long, bewildering drive in the dark. The battalion transport officer met us in the assembly area at Ripapersico and led us out into an open, sloping field, where we dug ourselves shallow slits. The platoon commanders were called to a small building, and it was arranged that company commanders would take it in turns to issue their orders.

John Reed explained our task with the aid of a map. The canal ran directly across our front. We were to cross by a bridge the sappers had constructed in the early hours, penetrate as far as the village of il Quartiere about a mile to the left on the other side and advance north along the road at first light. For support there would be a troop of tanks from the Bays. As for artillery, if we needed help, a call for a 'stonk' would bring down a thousand shells on the target area.

In another corner of the room Teddy Giles was giving out his orders. I noticed Chips there. He was scribbling notes and tracing the route on a tattered map with a grimy finger. He had even put on a pair of army spectacles with flat lenses and metal frames. It seemed somehow incongruous that this man, who had faced so much in life and experienced every privation and atrocity that war could produce, should be following the proceedings with such routine application. Yet, within the fateful sweep of war the perspective of the individual remained confined and precise; there was no choice but to focus on the narrow technicalities of one's allotted task.

After a shivery hour in our slit trenches we moved section by section down the track towards the canal. My platoon was leading. We scuttled rapidly over the bridge, turned left along the canal bank and then struck out through the open fields towards the village. We had planned to follow a line of electric cables which was marked on the map, but the line diverged into two lines and we took the wrong one. In the middle of a freshly-ploughed field we decided we had lost our way. It was an eerie experience wandering aimlessly about this silent, exposed, no man's land. At one point there was a sudden outburst from our own artillery. It was a short but heavy barrage and the shells came singing overhead to burst fiercely not far to our front. They seemed ominously close.

We stumbled on an underground shelter and I banged on the wooden door. '*Momento*,' I thundered down. The people inside stirred hastily, afraid of being massacred if they did not speak up. Two trembling peasants in night clothes came to the doorway. I asked them the way to the village. They pointed out the direction eagerly and added '*Si, si! vicino*', to our considerable relief. Then they peered at us intently and one of them asked, '*Tedeschi?*' '*No! Inglesi*,' I answered. Now they were beside themselves with joy. They woke their friends and rushed out to embrace us. We had to push them back into the shelter to shut them up.

Soon we reached the village and began to make our way between the buildings. The Lancashire Fusiliers were already there. We saw two men digging a trench in a front garden. 'Where's your company headquarters?' I called. They pointed to a house further down the road. It had been converted into a first aid post and casualties were being bandaged in the dim light of candles and torches. The company commander was standing at the door. 'Good morning,' I said. 'I've got to get in touch with you. We are passing through at first light.' 'OK, old boy,' he replied.

He had the normal haggard appearance of a tired commander but he looked unusually worn, with the vacant expression of someone who had just suffered a severe shock. He was silent for a few moments, and then the words welled up inside him and he spoke as though he couldn't keep them down. 'There's been a bog up. Did you hear that last stonk? Some bloody fool called it down on top of my front platoon.'

'Many hurt?' I asked. 'About a dozen. They were in the open – they didn't have a chance.' He fell silent and seemed to be driving his horror within himself. His self-control was almost frightening. He turned slowly back into the room.

I called the platoon together and we made for a nearby house, the men pilfering eggs on the way for breakfast. Meanwhile more troops from the battalion joined us. The machine gun platoon established itself in the canal bank and started to pump a confident stream of bullets down the flanks. The Germans retaliated with their *Nebelwerfer*. In the distance we could hear the horrible creaking, grinding sound, like some gigantic pump handle; and then the bombs fell around us, setting fire to the haystacks outside.

As dawn was breaking the tank commander from the Bays arrived and introduced himself. We discussed the forthcoming advance with the delicate, genteel bargaining that always took place between tank and infantry: myself, hoping to persuade the tanks to go in front; he, politely determined that they should not. The infantryman considered the tank an overpowering leviathan, which should be hurled indiscriminately into the assault; the tank man looked on the infantry as a convenient expendable mass useful for neutralising anti-tank guns. We managed to come to a working agreement.

Soon the go-ahead was given and we set off through the village. But almost at once fresh orders arrived: 'Turn about and march back. . . . The plan has been changed. The CO has decided he will not get through along the road.' Instead 'D' Company and No.4 Company were to launch an attack obliquely across our front. They were starting from the rear, and would by-pass the village. By now we could already see the two companies moving forward through the trees with tanks and carriers, and hear confused rifle and machine-gun fire in the distance. 'A' Company was hauled back into reserve, taking up position on the edge of the canal, which was filled with scummy, stagnant water.

In front of us was a long, low barn, which was the battalion tactical headquarters for this particular attack. I went inside to listen to the progress of the battle over the wireless. No.4 Company were meeting heavy opposition and there were a number of casualties. Teddy Giles was calling for Red Cross jeeps and carriers. A runner arrived and the news flashed round: 'Mr Louis is killed.' His head was blown off, somebody said. The men were aghast. Chips had previously served in 'A' Company and they knew him well. To them he had been the embodiment of indestructibility; and now he was dead.

Later there were further confused reports of counter-attacks and heavy enemy sniping, until Teddy Giles came on the set again. His voice was solid and defiant. 'Have taken all objectives. Shall I push on?' The CO decided to make a reconnaissance himself and told Teddy to wait. He went off on foot with two or three others.

I lay in the barn for the rest of that hot afternoon amid the smell of manure, a group of German prisoners in one corner, the wounded in the other, and the wireless with tinny monotony spluttering out confused and alarming reports. The CO had been gone almost an hour. His wireless had broken down and no message had been received. It was learned that the party had not reached No. 4 Company. After a while there were serious fears for their safety. The battalion second-in-command had arrived meanwhile. Major Fisher, known as 'Vino', was a highly experienced campaigner, but when he was told he would have to take over the battalion he protested, 'But I'm not in the picture. I'm not in the picture!'

At length the lost party turned up safe and sound. They had been intercepted on the way and badly sniped; they had escaped only by crawling on all fours for several hundred yards through a field of long grass. Now they were laughing with relief. The colonel had good news. 'Settle down beside the barn for the night. There'll be no move before dawn.' This was a comfort at any rate. The slit trenches were already dug, so we filled them with straw and crawled inside.

Suddenly a cry arose, 'Get dressed. We're moving forward in ten minutes.' I felt distinctly guilty about the way the men had been misled, albeit unintentionally. But they buckled to promptly and apart from a chorus of spontaneous expletives took it philosophically. They were used to it. In fact, to the private soldier, this is what the business was all about. When everyone was dressed we moved forward, following the route we had seen the other companies take earlier in the day. We found 'D' Company in a large farm building, with carriers and jeeps parked in the yard. The men were lining up for a meal.

John Reed was waiting with orders for a company attack on

an isolated house about eight hundred yards away. It was a clear and cloudless night and as we filed along a ditch towards the open fields the vines on the banks above shone like skeletons in the moonlight. There was not a sound as we closed on our objective. The Germans had evidently withdrawn. We rushed the house, battered open the doors and forced our way in. It was empty. But there was a *rifugio* in the garden and we could hear moaning inside. The shelter had received a direct hit from our artillery and a group of Italian civilians, men and women, were writhing in a heap on the floor. Two were dead, some others badly wounded and the rest very shocked. In another shelter we found two more casualties. The wounded Italians were dumb, petrified and bleeding. We led them into the house, bandaged them by torchlight and persuaded them to be evacuated on our stretchers.

Orders came to dig in around the house. At this the men rebelled. It was about the tenth time they had been required to dig in within twenty-four hours, and they were sick of it. Everyone was weary and fed up. However, we dug token slits as a gesture and posted sentries. The company commander then called me into the house with orders for a patrol. There was a road half a mile across country to the east, and on this I was to meet the forward elements of the divisional recce regiment, who would shortly be arriving. I walked across with one man. The area was quite empty. The two of us waited in a ditch, but there was no sign of the recce unit. After an hour I returned in disgust to report that no one had appeared. But the CO was insistent on contact being made. I cursed and argued with John for some minutes, for we needed sleep. But I had to go. I returned grudgingly, alone, as I couldn't bring myself to keep anyone else awake on such a tiresome mission. At last I spotted the armoured cars arriving, and after a few words with the leading troop commander returned to the company.

Next morning an old Italian peasant, the father of the family, came back to the house. He had been held up overnight and separated from the others; now he returned to see the disaster that had overtaken his household – his mother, wife and children all killed or maimed, and his home reduced to a pile of rubble. He was distraught as he ran wildly about the house, wailing like a demented character in some classical drama. He would not be comforted and we could only stand by and watch him in the transports of his grief. There was nothing one could do for him.

In the late afternoon we moved forward again, a mile or so along a hedge. On the path we found some leaflets which had been dropped by the Germans. On one side they were like holiday brochures, with a picture of three bathing belles surrounded by baskets of luscious fruits. The caption read: 'British soldiers welcome to the River Po.' But on the back was a grim, black death's-head skeleton with the words: 'This is what is waiting for you on the other side!'

The track ran over a slight rise through an orchard smothered in pink fruit blossom and down to a little village. There was some shelling and mortaring, but nothing fell near us and we soon reached the safety of the buildings. Orders arrived for a further attack. There was another canal in front. 'D' Company had tried to cross, but were pinned down. 'B' Company, however, had succeeded in seizing a bridge a mile further downstream to the left. We were to pass through 'B' Company and, by attacking from a flank, take the original 'D' Company objective, a group of houses on the other side of the canal in the village of Runco.

We pressed on through the gathering darkness by a roundabout route and swung across the broken bridge over the canal, where 'B' Company had formed their bridgehead. Their company headquarters was in a spacious building. Inside, despite the general turmoil and tension, we were greeted with serene imperturbability by 'Windy' Squire, who was now in command. We studied our objectives from maps and air photographs, and one of the platoon commanders took us outside and pointed them out on the ground. The first objective was a large farmhouse which had been shelled by our artillery and the surrounding barns and haystacks set on fire. Through the crackling flames we could just make out the silhouettes of the buildings behind.

When the order for the attack was given the sections deployed, the men fixed bayonets and we burst through the hedge out into the open field. We raced through the blazing haystacks and outbuildings among the flickering shadows and billowing smoke, our weapons at the alert; but there was no opposition. The main farmhouse, which looked like an enormous barrack block, proved empty. The Germans had pulled out again. We searched the buildings quickly and passed on to the village behind. There was no one there either. This was the finish of Eight Platoon's task; we picked our house, a whitewashed cottage undamaged and deserted, and forced open the locked doors.

From the yard a soldier called out, 'Someone down here, sir.' He pointed to a shelter in the garden. From inside came the sound of heavy snoring. I tossed a brick into the shelter and shouted, 'Come on out!' The snoring ceased. There was a sudden flustered scuffle, as though someone was making a dash for it. I put a burst of tommy-gun fire through the open door to be on the safe side. Out staggered an enormous pig, snorting and squealing, with blood pouring from its back. A quick shot from one of the men's Bren guns put the old creature out of his agony.

Meanwhile, Dennis Smith had passed through with his platoon. They were to clear the canal bank behind us. They captured three prisoners and brought them back to the cottage. John Reed arrived shortly afterwards with his company headquarters. The cottage was soon packed and there was quite a hubbub, with the company commander bellowing unsuccessfully into the wireless and the rest of us chattering blithely together. In the middle of the pandemonium a dear old Italian lady, who must have been at least ninety, arrived, presumably with the object of turning us out of her house. She made very little impression, for no one could make out a word she was saying. The only composed person in the room was a tall, saucy German prisoner, who stood in the background smiling sardonically at this spectacle of British confusion.

In the morning there was the usual invasion, with battalion headquarters clamouring for the best billets and the Italians returning with an eye to their precious belongings. The latter were not a moment too soon, for one or two men had organised a regular postal service for the disposal of their loot, wrapping up clocks and other valuables and sending them back in the company jeep to the rear echelon, where they were posted home to England in a steady stream.

It was good to be safe again. The company was shifted back to the old farm buildings which had been our first objective on the previous night. The Italian owners had returned, but we negotiated with them for a couple of bedrooms. One of these was furnished with the most beautiful walnut bedroom suite, which seemed quite out of place in this simple farmstead. Unfortunately the outside wall had been struck by a shell and the furniture and bed were smothered in a fine red powder. But we were not unduly troubled. Four of us climbed in together to sleep. Sleep! It had ceased to be a mere matter of routine or a luxury; it was a brutal necessity, something we snatched at like starving men at a crust. No one could say when we should get another chance.

For a day and night we slept, ate, washed and refreshed ourselves with vino, and our energies and spirits were rapidly restored. The news from outside was splendid. The offensive was making good progress, and the armour had already reached the River Po. We were in no doubt ourselves that the fighting had shifted well forward, for a mobile workshop even arrived at the farm, a harbinger of blissful security indeed! Round about us the Italians were busy salvaging what they could from the ruins of the fire, which had destroyed their crops, barns and haystacks. It always seemed to be the men who stood about hopelessly, bewailing their misfortunes, while the women busied themselves making good the damage.

16

At breakfast-time on the morning of 23 April the company was ordered to resume the advance by transport. The route took us a long way forward, through country which was quite undamaged, so swift had been the advance. Solemn little groups of Italians stood outside their houses applauding as we passed. In due course we dismounted and continued on foot. The colour-sergeant arrived with haversack rations for the midday meal and set up a stall by the roadside. As each man trudged past he handed out two doorsteps of bread and margarine and a hunk of cheese. Most of the men couldn't be bothered to put the ration away in their haversacks and ate it as they marched down the road.

The column halted at Viconovo in a field of clover by yet another river, the Po di Volano. The Northamptons had already crossed, leaving a couple of assault boats in the water, with wire cables attached to pickets in the bank. We took it in turns to paddle across the sluggish ochre-coloured stream in the flimsy canvas craft. After clambering up the soggy slope on the opposite side we stumbled forward in open order across a wide, ploughed field.

Ahead was a steep roadside bank, where the Northamptons had dug in. We lay down, some on the bank and some in a belt of crops behind. It was a gloriously sunny morning with a silence that was disarming. Suddenly an enemy shell burst behind us. We all fell flat, the more fortunate diving into slits with the Northamptons. Five more shells followed from an enemy self-propelled gun; they came whining gently overhead, each one following the other after a short pause. Their sound had a peculiar caressing mockery, as though they were playfully reluctant to land, until their flight terminated in a slithering rush and a grating splatter as the singing fragments hissed over us. Then all was quiet. I raised my head. There was a cry for stretcher-bearers from the next platoon. Three men were borne away to the rear. One of them was writhing badly and the orderlies could not carry him. As they passed they appealed to me for help. I detailed someone to hold him down by force on the stretcher.

Soon we moved forward into Fossalta, flitting from doorway to doorway along the dozen or so houses which lined the street. The village was deserted, with the unnatural air of a place under enemy observation. The whole company squeezed into the last house before the open road. Our way lay along a narrow country lane with a hedge on each side. This curved forward towards the town of Tamara, which stood on a road junction, our last objective before the Po. The company's task was to penetrate to the outskirts, so that the battalion could occupy the rest of the town after dark.

We had about half a mile to go; but there were occasional houses at intervals along the lane, and it was a question of leapfrogging from one to the other. On each side were open, flat, cultivated fields, interspersed with low hedges and a few trees. Towards the east everything was quiet; but from the west, near Ferrara, came a confused noise of firing and battle. The recce regiment was said to be making good progress alongside us. They, too, were to converge on Tamara by nightfall. I also noticed a patrol from the Irish Brigade probing around a flank. This superabundance of troops was a sure sign of a highly successful operation.

Dennis Smith and his platoon took the first house; there was no resistance. Eight Platoon passed through to the next, covering the intervening ground swiftly. The building was in good condition, unshelled, with window-panes intact and furniture undamaged; there were even books open on a table. The curtains were blowing gently. The house, though empty, had the appearance of having been occupied until a few moments before our arrival and then abruptly deserted. Two fine horses were trotting round in the field outside. The men crowded into the rooms. The more restless wandered upstairs looting.

We peered through the upstairs window towards the next large house, about three hundred yards away. It seemed silent and harmless. Someone thought he spotted a German in a slit trench near the next house, and there was a good deal of gesticulating and arguing. Norris, a spirited soldier who had just rejoined the platoon after a spell away, wanted to go down the ditch after him with grenades, but I dissuaded him. Instead, Webb took a Bren to the front window and gave the trench a thorough pasting. There was a pause. Then an abrupt and spiteful response came from the enemy. Spandau bullets splattered through the window against the wall behind, and a concentration of artillery shells burst around the house. The air was heavy with sudden violence. Those of us near the windows fell flat on our faces; the others scurried downstairs.

Then it was quiet again. The ground outside was pitted with smoking shell-holes and the two horses lay dead in the field. John Reed came doubling into the house with company headquarters. One of our tanks arrived and from a corner of the building began to direct streams of incendiary bullets towards the enemy. Soon the haystacks and surrounding buildings were ablaze, and vast screens of thick grey smoke were swept across the road and fields by the stiff breeze. An enemy self-propelled gun, seeking out our tank, fired a round of solid shot. It struck the wall of the house with a tremendous impact that made the building ring and stirred up a fog of thick red dust that left us blinded and choking. There was a startled exodus from the front rooms to the back of the house. As the dust cloud cleared and we could see each other again, two men were brought in bleeding from head wounds.

Dennis was told to take the next house. He and his platoon crossed quickly without harm. Through the smoke we could see them entering the building. The men winkled out about seven Germans, who surrendered without a fight. I was ordered to pass through Dennis's platoon and take the next three houses, which stood close together on the outskirts of the village. The smoke was thinning and we could see the buildings clearly. We had to cross a space of open ground. The tank man asked whether I wanted any support. 'Not unless we are fired on,' I told him. I had seen Dennis cross safely and was confident we could do the same.

I began to get the platoon ready. John came up and interjected, 'There's a message from the CO to get cracking. He says we're holding up the advance of the whole brigade.' 'I'm going as fast as I can. What the hell does he think we are?' I was suddenly angry and intolerant of all this safe, smug pressure from behind, urging my platoon on to destruction. It was always the same. They were in such a hell of a rush to write you off. I felt irrationally contemptuous of everyone in the army who was not taking part in this particular attack.

I gave a few hurried orders to the corporals and we were off, moving rapidly along the ditch to within fifty yards of the enemy houses. We grouped together for a quick dash over the road. I crossed safely into the ditch on the other side with the first section. The others were slow in following and I yelled at them to get a move on. 'Machine gun,' shouted one of them pointing down the road. 'It's quite safe,' I called. But they still hesitated. I decided to go back and fetch them. I scrambled quickly onto the roadway and straightened up to sprint across.

There was a burst of fire from very close, and I knew something had happened. It was hard at first to make out exactly what, but I felt strangely shocked. For a second everything seemed far away and misty; then all was vivid and real again. It was as though someone had awakened me from a dream by giving my leg a sharp tug and spun me round. 'I've been hit.' Glancing down, I saw a faint trickle of blood appearing through my trouser leg and dripping down my ankle on to the road, where it formed tiny crimson globules in the dust. My leg gave way and I collapsed to the ground.

I called to the men in the ditch opposite me. They were watching, fearful of further shooting. Then Norris jumped up. He pulled me upright and heaved me on to his shoulder. 'If they fire again, we've had it,' he muttered. As he stumbled forward, I cried out in pain. 'Put me down, for God's sake put me down in the ditch.' But Norris went on. A few minutes later Sergeant Peers arrived and together they carried me into the house.

The men were already inside. They looked startled. They did not like to see an officer hit. One of them took off my anklet and began to pull off my boot. It hurt. 'Look out! He's fainting,' someone said. I slithered to the ground. They propped me up with pillows and put shell dressings on my leg. I did not look at the wound. It was so comforting to be entirely in someone else's hands. 'I'm sorry, you blokes, to leave you like this,' I stammered. Then, collecting my thoughts, I added, 'You mustn't wait here with me. You must push on.' They explained that Sergeant Peers was looking for Mr Smith and had told them to wait until he got back.

The signaller wirelessed for a stretcher. In a matter of moments the stretcher-bearers arrived. For some reason there were four of them. They lifted me up and I was borne on high, like an emperor in triumph. They walked calmly down the middle of the road, with me waving the Red Cross flag, which I volunteered to carry. I felt no pain at all from the wound so long as I was lying still. In company headquarters John said, 'Thank God it's not worse.' The company sergeant-major gave me a cigarette. 'A nice Blighty one, I should say, sir.' He seemed genuinely envious.

A doctor arrived with a stretcher jeep. He was the medical officer of the tank unit supporting us, a little man wearing an American-type steel helmet. He was brisk and attentive. When my stretcher was loaded aboard he drove away, stopping further down the road to pick up another casualty. 'How are you feeling?' he asked me. 'It's all right when the jeep isn't moving,' I told him, 'but it hurts like hell going over the bumps.' He came round and examined the leg. 'I'm not surprised,' he said. He put on a splint, bound a fresh bandage over the leg and gave me a jab above the knee with a morphia capsule.

We drove back to the regimental aid post, which had been set up in the village church near battalion headquarters at Fossalta. Inside, 'Doc' Miedema was busy tending the wounded in his shirt-sleeves. He decided that my splint and dressing were adequate. 'Vino' Fisher, who was temporarily in command of the battalion, and Geoffrey Rose, the intelligence officer, had also looked in to offer sympathy as I lay and sipped tea from an enamel mug. When the ambulance arrived I was carried from the church.

The afternoon sun was now quite low in the sky and the village buildings were casting lengthening shadows across the dusty road. Away to the front there still sounded bursts of machine-gun fire and the desultory explosions of shells. The stretcher was lifted into the vehicle by two orderlies and carefully strapped to a bunk inside. 'That's it, then,' said one of them, adding with a grin as he backed towards the door, 'You'll be between clean sheets tonight, sir.' As the orderlies climbed down the steps to the ground I caught a last glimpse over their shoulders of sections of troops in single file threading their way slowly forward through the medley of vehicles dispersed around the headquarters. Then the doors were slammed shut and my sojourn with the East Surreys came to its premature close.

Index: Places

Index: People

Adams, Cpl, East Surreys 168

Beecher, Lt V.A., Welch 33
Blunden, Lt G., Royal Sussex 113, 141, 145
Bridgeman, L/Cpl, Royal Sussex 65–67, 70, 75, 81, 88
Brooks, Sgt, Royal Sussex 90
Bull, Sgt, Welch 15, 20, 23
Butcher, Cpl, East Surreys 168

Cairncross, Lt N.F., Royal Sussex 79, 109, 120
Campbell, Capt E.M., Royal Sussex 46
Climpson, Pte 54, 57
Cobb, Pte E., Royal Sussex 88, 133
Cross, Pte R., Royal Sussex 71, 80, 82, 84, 85, 100

Dishman, Lt V.L., Royal Sussex (South Staffs) 107, 126
Duke, Pte, Royal Sussex 70

Evans, Lt P.R., Royal Sussex 108, 109

Fisher, Major M.E., East Surreys (Royal Warwicks) 177, 186
Freeman, Lt C.D., Royal Sussex 107, 133

Gates, Lt R.A., East Surreys (RA) 148, 163
Giles, Capt E.H., East Surreys 148, 149, 154, 155, 165, 169, 174, 176, 177

Halsall, Capt J.A.L., Royal Sussex 64, 66, 74, 75, 79, 81, 83, 86–8, 91, 92, 100
Henderson, Pte, Royal Sussex 88
Hinkins, Pte S., Royal Sussex 104, 133
Homden, Sgt, Royal Sussex 74
Hooper, Lt-Colonel K.C., Royal Sussex (Queens) 52
Horsley, Lt R.H., Royal Sussex 107, 111
Howe, Lt J., Manchesters 45, 49, 53, 58, 59–62, 63
Hunter, Lt-Colonel H.M.A., East Surreys (Northamptons) 154

Jelley, Capt G.M., Royal Sussex 64, 92, 125
Johnson, Cpl, Royal Sussex 65, 75, 83, 84
Jones, Pte R., Welch 17

Kitson, Capt J.D., Royal Sussex (Devons) 108, 109

Lacey, Lt E.R., South Wales Borderers 57, 58
Lee, Capt W.M., Royal Sussex 62, 63
Ledger, Lt J.W.C., East Surreys (Cheshires) 161, 167

Louis, Lt J.F., East Surreys 165, 166, 169, 174, 176, 177

Mahon, Pte, Royal Sussex 88, 90, 133
Martin, Lt J.F., Royal Sussex 104, 105
McCully, Lt-Colonel J.J., Royal Sussex 83, 129
Mendelsohn, Pte J., Welch 17, 20, 28
Miedema, Capt J., East Surreys (RAMC) 148, 185

Norris, Pte E., East Surreys 183–185

Parsons, Pte, East Surreys 166, 174
Peers, Sgt, East Surreys 185
Pett, Pte, Royal Sussex 70

Rafferty, Pte J., Welch 17, 19, 20, 28
Reed, Major F.J., East Surreys 155, 162, 165, 168, 169, 172, 174, 177, 178, 180,
    183–5
Richards, Capt D., Royal Sussex 86, 126
Robinson, Major P.N., East Surreys (RA) 148
Rose, Lt G.T., East Surreys (Queens) 186
Rose, Pte, Royal Sussex 85

Salter, Lt H.J.R., Royal Sussex (Royal Hampshires) 133
Saunders, Major J.A.H., East Surreys 155
Shearer, Sgt, East Surreys 160
Smart, Pte, East Surreys 170
Smith, Lt D.J., East Surreys (RA) 148, 180, 183–85
Squire, Capt G.L.A., East Surreys 149, 179

Templer, Brig, G.W.R. 33
True, L/Cpl, East Surreys 168
Tyler, Major A.C., Welch 19, 20

Webb, Pte J., East Surreys 160, 166, 183
White, Sgt H., Royal Sussex 74

Note: Parent regiments shown in brackets

Index: Units